UNAUTHORIZED AND UNCENSORED

The Next Generation
TRIBUTE

BOOK TWO

EDITED BY
JAMES VAN HISE

A PIONEER BOOK

Recently Released Pioneer Books. . .

MTV: MUSIC YOU CAN SEE	ISBN#1-55698-355-7
TREK: THE NEXT GENERATION CREW BOOK	ISBN#1-55698-363-8
TREK: THE PRINTED ADVENTURES	ISBN#1-55698-365-5
THE CLASSIC TREK CREW BOOK	ISBN#1-55698-368-9
TREK VS THE NEXT GENERATION	ISBN#1-55698-370-0
TREK: THE NEXT GENERATION TRIBUTE BOOK	ISBN#1-55698-366-2
THE HOLLYWOOD CELEBRITY DEATH BOOK	ISBN#1-55698-369-7
LET'S TALK: AMERICA'S FAVORITE TV TALK SHOW HOSTS	ISBN#1-55698-364-6
HOT-BLOODED DINOSAUR MOVIES	ISBN#1-55698~365-4
BONANZA: THE UNOFFICIAL STORY OF THE PONDEROSA	ISBN#1-55698-359-X

Exciting new titles soon to be released

THE KUNG FU BOOK	ISBN#1-55698-328-X
TREK: THE DEEP SPACE CELEBRATION	ISBN#1-55698 330-1
TREK: THE DEEP SPACE CREW BOOK	ISBN#1-55698-335-2
MARRIAGE & DIVORCE -HOLLYWOOD STYLE	ISBN#1-55698-333-6
TREK: THE ENCYCLOPEDIA	ISBN#1-55698-331-X
THE LITTLE HOUSE COMPANION	ISBN#1-55698-332-8

PUBLISHER: Hal Schuster   **DESIGNER:** Ben Long   **EDITOR:** Chuck Sperry

Library of Congress Cataloging-in-Publication Data
James Van Hise, 1959—

Next Generation Tribute Book Two

1. Next Generation Tribute Book Two (television, popular culture)
I. Title

Published by Pioneer Books, Inc., 5715 N. Balsam Rd., Las Vegas, NV, 89130.

First Printing, 1994

TABLE OF CONTENTS

WITHER THE NEXT GENERATION?

Seven years. That's a long time for any television series to be on the air. The dream of most producers is to have their series last just five years. Paramount's original stated goal for THE NEXT GENERATION was six years, but they decided to continue it for another season due to the demands of the TV stations who air the series. They aren't the only ones who want the series to keep delivering 25 new episodes a year; so do the fan and some of the cast members.

Now it looks as though the cast of THE NEXT GENERATION will be picking up the mantle from the original STAR TREK and carrying it into a series of motion pictures. This looks like it may not be the same approach used in the previous Trek movies. Rather than one film every two years or so, one of the producers of TNG has privately suggested that they may appear more often. What will decide?

In February 1994 Viacom emerged as the victor in the bid to acquire Paramount. They will ultimately decide what form and how frequently STAR TREK—THE NEXT GENERA-

TION will appear after 1994. When it was any-body's guess who would emerge the victor among the warring bids for Paramount, the industry trade paper VARIETY suggested that the new owners might rethink concluding the TV version of NEXT GENERATION after seven years. After all, Paramount's successful series CHEERS ran for eleven years. Rumors abound, but they'll settle into a course by the end of 1994.

Whatever the future holds, NEXT GENERA-TION has emerged as the fan favorite in the STAR TREK universe. Clearly it has supplanted the original STAR TREK in the hearts and minds of many fans.

The larger-than-life characterizations of Kirk, Spock and McCoy may yet become the source for another STAR TREK spin-off. New actors may step into those now-legendary roles as STAR TREK comes full circle, back to where it began.

That's the thing about the future: Anything is possible.

—*James Van Hise*

ON THE SET OF THE NEXT GENERATION WITH "GOOD MORNING AMERICA"

[or How Come Nobody Is Saying Anything About Patrick Stewart's Notable Absence?]

It is rare for a news magazine show to have complete access to the sets of a popular TV series. The following report of what happened when GOOD MORNING AMERICA had such access may explain why it isn't done more often.

It was February 13th, 1992 when the ABC production crew of GOOD MORNING AMERICA beamed out to Los Angeles. GOOD MORNING AMERICA usually beamed its broadcasts from its New York City studios. But the show periodically went cruising through space in order to shake up its stayed format. Unfortunately, whenever it attempted this feat, the GOOD MORNING AMERICA crew exhibited all of the flaws inherent in its vehicle and similar morning magazine shows. The show was broadcast that day from Paramount Studios, from the actual sets of STAR TREK—THE NEXT GENERATION. They had a good idea —they just didn't know what to do with the idea when it was realized.

The show opened with co-host Charles Gibson stating, "Good morning, America, from the USS Enterprise, home to the cast of STAR TREK—THE NEXT GENERATION." Gibson and co-host Joan Lunden introduced themselves and announced that this was the fourth day of their Great Hollywood Wake-Up Tour.

"And we're on the bridge, which is really neat," Joan tried to gush inarticulately. "There's neat stuff around here on the Enterprise."

"It is 1992. But we really come to you from the 24th century," Gibson said solemnly as the red-alert sounded in the distance.

He looked around as if wondering whether Joan had somehow tripped the alarm. "They know we're here; I think they've spotted us. But we are going to be on the sets, really, of STAR TREK—THE NEXT GENERATION through the day."

"And there's a lot of them!" Joan insisted, speaking of the sets.

"We have a little model here of the Enterprise, as it is supposed to be like. Theoretically the ship is half a mile long, and theoretically we are right here in the top; that's where the bridge is located. But in

reality the USS Enterprise is really about a dozen sets," Gibson revealed, "scattered around three sound stages here on the Paramount lot.

"For instance, the Ten Forward lounge, that's supposed to be ten decks down and in the front of the ship—in truth it's about twenty-five feet over here," he said, gesturing to one side of the sound stage. "But the detail on this set, on the bridge, is really amazing. For instance, back here where the crew sits, the control seats, they all swivel, and there's some very authen-

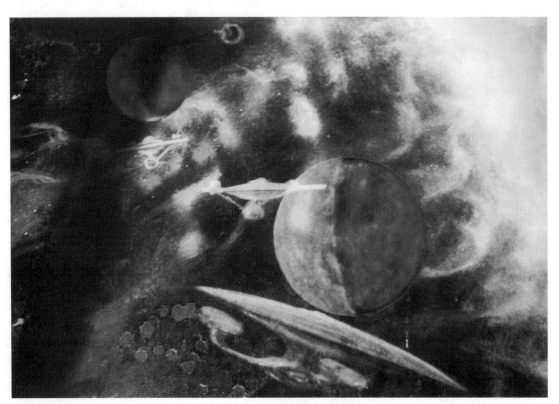

Hanging on the wall of Beverly Crusher's office, is this painting of the various incarnations of the Enterprise.

Photo c 1994 by "Deep Focus"

tic looking things, here, built into the arms. I love the way these control panels swivel around, and you can use them just about any which way."

Gibson then pointed out the dedication plaque on the wall, rarely seen in the episodes themselves, which dedicates when and where the Enterprise was built

"It says, here, it was launched Stardate 40759.5 which I'm told translates to year 2363. That's when the ship was launched: made in the Utopia Planetia Fleet Yards in Mars. Where else would it be built?"

Then he explained that they would be moving around the dozen sets, and Joan Lunden pointed out that they'd also be talking to the entire cast in the "intergalactic lounge," or so they believed then. Unfortunately, something would happen, behind the scenes. . . but more on that later.

INCLEMENT WEATHER AND AN ASTRONAUT

In spite of being broadcast directly from the NEXT GENERATION sets, GOOD MORNING AMERICA still featured its usual quota of news and spotlighted 1992's catastrophic winter rainstorm. The storm pelted Los Angeles, caused massive flooding throughout the region, even directly affected the broadcast itself. It was the worst rain storm of the century to strike Southern California. GOOD MORNING AMERICA has a hokey tradition: celebrities wish America good morning. The first of these came from former astronaut Alan Shepard, who stated, "As America's first man in space, let me express my very best wishes to the crew of the USS Enterprise as they explore new galaxies and unknown worlds. Good morning, America!" The theme from STAR TREK—THE NEXT GENERATION played in the background of his mes-

sage.

Returning to the hosts, Charles Gibson and Joan Lunden observed how nice it was for Shepard to give that personal message to the STAR TREK cast. "So many of the astronauts — apparently — are big fans of STAR TREK," Gibson stated, "and it is interesting that many of the cast were inspired by the astronauts. One of the cast members, that I'm going to be talking to in this half hour, Michael Dorn who plays one of the Klingons, Lt. Werf (sic)— I believe —wanted to be an astronaut when he was a kid. It didn't happen, but he got the next best thing which is to be in this cast."

"SNAZZY DIGS"

Charles Gibson actually did call him "Werf" which made one wonder whether he had ever seen THE NEXT GENERATION. Certainly the cast sitting backstage must have groaned over that one. It was comparable to the common mistake the original STAR TREK cast encountered when Mr. Spock was often referred to as "Dr. Spock" by the media.

"The next best thing for us, though," Joan continued, ignoring the faux pas made by her co-host, "is to be making this our backdrop this morning, and these are some rather snazzy digs." Joan was never at a loss for a colorful expression, particularly if it was a cliché.

"These are the guest accommodations on the USS Enterprise," Gibson continued as they entered the set for one of the crew quarters, a set which is redressed and rearranged depending upon whose quarters it is meant to represent in a particular episode being filmed. "We're going to be talking about where we are. It is interesting that on these very sound stages on the Paramount lot, the original STAR TREK was made here. And they use it still for STAR TREK—THE NEXT GENERATION. But there is so much histo-

ry on the Paramount lot," he explained. "It's interesting that these studios that grew up in the movie age now devote so many of their resources to television. I guess that's sort of a sign of the times.

"But on this Paramount lot, three thousand movies were made in all, including the first Best Picture Academy Award winner, WINGS, all the GODFATHERs, THE TEN COMMANDMENTS were made here; also the Indiana Jones movies were made here."

AN IMPOSTER ABOARD THE ENTERPRISE

Then came another news segment. And when they returned, the weather man, Spencer Christian, was seen wearing a Starfleet uniform and sitting at the bar in Ten Forward. He was being served by an actor in full Romulan makeup, apparently from the episode being filmed there that day. Making a joke when the Romulan served him,

the weatherman stated, "Hmm, that doesn't look like coffee. What is this?"

"Gorgon stomach extract," the Romulan soberly replied.

"I see. Regular or decaffeinated?"

"Both," the Romulan replied.

"Great way to start the morning, with Gorgon stomach extract. Here's looking at you," Christian stated as he picked up the cup to drink. Then they cut away to a commercial. They returned with a short history of the studio, well known for producing all the versions of STAR TREK.

This segment began by showing classic behind-the-scenes footage of old Hollywood stars Gary Cooper and Harpo Marx walking around on the backlot. Then the man behind the creation of Paramount, Adolph Zucker, was profiled. Zucker ran Paramount for most of his 103 years of life.

"And he hired a director who understood the concept of big," Joan

Lunden explained as she introduced a clip showing Cecil B. DeMille. "Oscar entered the picture in 1929, when Paramount's WINGS won the first Academy Award for Best Picture." Then clips from other classic Paramount films were shown featuring performers Mae West, the Marx Brothers, Alan Ladd, Gloria Swanson, Bob Hope and Bing Crosby. After interviewing a man who has worked at Paramount since 1937, they did a transition to

Photo c 1994 Albert L. Ortega

contemporary Hollywood and the box-office stars who currently work on the lot. Harrison Ford and Ann Archer were shown making PATRIOT GAMES. They mentioned other shows — CHEERS, STAR TREK—THE NEXT GENERATION and ARSENIO HALL.

A SUPERFICIAL HISTORY

GOOD MORNING AMERICA's presentation of Paramount history was sketchy at best. Segments were as complete as they could make them between commercial breaks which wasn't that complete. This resulted in a jumpy quality as GOOD MORNING

Levar Burton at the Bonaventure Hotel Creation Convention's Q&A with cast. March 15, 91.

Photo c 1994 Albert L. Ortega

AMERICA lurched from one subject to the next, from one set to the next, and from one interview to the next. The interviews with the performers are brief and superficial. It was as though all the stars of STAR TREK—THE NEXT GENERATION were chatting like chums with the hosts, and that was more than enough. They were not given much time to say anything, and this was apparently beside the point.

Joan Lunden interviewed Jonathan Frakes, Marina Sirtis and Brent Spiner. The questions were routine; Joan pointed out that Brent is usually in gold makeup which takes about an hour and fifteen minutes to apply. But the actors were all in their street clothes for the interviews. When Brent was asked if his makeup does anything to his skin because of how often he wears it, Spiner replied, "I don't know what it's doing inside. Basically I think one day they're going to find my organs; roaches and my organs are going to be the only thing left after a holocaust."

Lunden observed that it would have been easy for Paramount to make the show a space age Western, but the studio had more vision than that.

"We like to think so," Jonathan replied. "Certainly, we attack more things than aliens on the show."

THE REAL SPACEMEN

The actors were asked if they'd like to go into space—for real—given the chance. Spiner was the first to reply, "If it's first class."

Joan said she'd been told that Marina wouldn't go. The actress explained, "No, I don't like heights. I get vertigo up real high, so I don't think I would go. I'm a coward."

"I'm there," Jonathan stated. "I'm ready to go!"

The STAR TREK cast had met some of the original astronauts; Joan wanted to know what the astronauts thought of the actors.

"Bill Dana's very fond of us," Frakes deadpanned. He was referring to the little remembered '60s comedian who played the character Jose Jimenez, Mexico's fearful astronaut.

Joan pointed out that some of the new astronauts said they were inspired by STAR TREK. "They all say that," Frakes replied. STAR TREK and its fans have long been supporters of NASA.

"I think you have to be so bright to get into [NASA]," Marina added. "I think that it is something that is in you; a gene almost that's in you. It would be flattering to think [we could join NASA], but it wouldn't be us anyway. It would be the original cast."

"They're the real cowboys," Frakes insisted.

NO TYPECASTING CONCERNS

Joan noted that the cast of the original STAR

TREK had become so closely identified with the show that they found it difficult to extend their careers beyond it. Frakes returned, "I'm thankful for the job I have."

But Marina added, "I think it is a valid point—actually—because we are actors, and we didn't become actors just to be on STAR TREK, obviously. But I don't think we're going to be as legendary as them, because they were the first. And they've been doing it for so long. I don't think in twenty-five years time we're still going to have our uniforms on."

With that the show broke away for a commercial and announced before cutting away that the first space shuttle ever tested was named the Enterprise after the original STAR TREK's starship. What they didn't say was that NASA opposed that name. They were overruled, and the space shuttle Enterprise performed flight tests and landings in the atmosphere. It never went into space.

Next came Charles Gibson with more cast members from STAR TREK—THE NEXT GENERATION, although Patrick Stewart wasn't in this group. He was the only cast member who didn't appear on the show, a fact never discussed the entire morning. Patrick Stewart was never mentioned at all, conspicuously omitted, but it wasn't until some weeks later that I learned why this was so.

MORE CAST INTERVIEWS

The other three cast members who were interviewed next were LeVar Burton, Gates McFadden and Michael Dorn.

Charles Gibson began by stating, "The USS Enterprise travels at warp

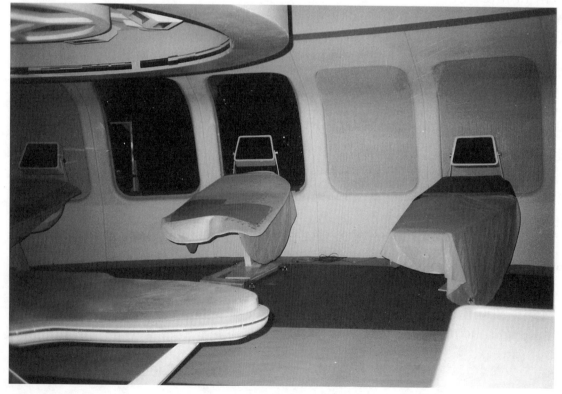

Sickbay.
Photo c 1994
"Deep Focus"

factor 9.6 in STAR TREK lingo. That is hundreds of times the speed of light, but it's never fast enough to keep the ship or its crew out of danger." A clip was shown from the episode "Disaster" which featured Dr. Crusher and Geordi LaForge, as well as a clip from another episode showing Worf. "Again in civilian dress joining us now, three more members of the cast."

The first question asked was—again—about makeup. This time it was addressed to Michael Dorn. Makeup for Worf takes 90 minutes to accomplish, Dorn replied.

Gibson asked LeVar Burton if he can see wearing his eye appliance.

"That's the irony," Burton explained. "I'm an actor playing a blind man who sees when he wears this device. Yet when I put it on about eighty percent of my vision is taken away." His peripheral vision is completely blocked. "I used to bump into things."

Gibson observed that all Gates McFadden had to do is put on the wig and the uniform and she'd be ready. She facetiously replied, "Yeah, yeah, there's no makeup at all for women." She pointed out that it took her an hour and fifteen minutes to do her makeup because her real long hair had to be pulled up and fastened in place in order to make room for the large hairpiece she wore as Dr. Crusher.

EYES ON THE STARS

Michael Dorn agreed that his makeup took about 90 minutes to do. "It started out to be about three hours, and I don't want to see when I get into makeup." As to whether it's good news or bad news that he's not recognized without his makeup, Dorn stated that it's fine with him. "I like the anonymity." But he agreed that people sometimes recognized his voice. "It's just that without the makeup they don't put it together. Most of the time they kind of look and they kind of stare and cock their head a little bit." He remarked that people sometimes ask him if he's James Earl Jones.

Charles Gibson walked around the set noticing a lot of things which were clearly done for the amusement of the cast and crew. He asked about these gags. "When you have this many people working on a cast there's got to be a lot of inside jokes. As I walked down the hall and looked at the visitor's quarters, there's a little room there for Lt. Luke Skywalker. Are there things that go on? Tell me about the accordion."

Gates explained, "That must be the day that. . . we have all of these bridge scenes where we're talking to aliens on a big blue screen and the aliens aren't really there when we're doing the scene. And at one point all of the crew were on the bridge and an alien was about to speak, and I just happened to have my son's little concertina. And I just started to play a song behind that to liven it up."

Asked if they were all fans of the original STAR TREK, Michael Dorn stated that he was and that he wanted to be an astronaut. "Yeah, for a long time. I used to send away the box-tops of cereals for the old Friendship 7 spacecraft and I'd put it together and fly it around the house and all that stuff. When I got of Draft age I found out I have an eye deficiency and you couldn't do it." The host observed that being on STAR TREK is the next best thing. "Plus you don't get hurt this way," Dorn added.

THE DOCTOR IS IN

After a commercial break the show returned with Joan Lunden and Charles Gibson on the set of the observation lounge with its huge windows looking out on the stars. Joan observed, "Look at it out there! You see the final frontier!" Then she added, "The late Gene Roddenberry, who really created this program, really believed that in the 24th

century there would be very, very little wood. It would be a precious commodity, so you don't see a lot of wood around," she said, pointing around the sets. "He was really astute about all those kind of little touches."

"Yes, he was," Charles Gibson agreed, "and the detail on this set is really amazing. And we're not moving at warp speed, because you can see all those stars out there. But maybe we'll pick up much of that speed a little bit later in the program." He pointed out that each of the studio sets they'd been visiting for a week have belonged to different networks. And STAR TREK— THE NEXT GENERA-TION was a syndicated, off-network show. Because of the unique, often syndicated, sources which now exist for television programming, the next half-hour of GOOD MORN-ING AMERICA would include a roundtable interview with the entertainment chiefs of ABC, CBS, NBC and Fox about the future of television. They

were to discuss the new kinds of programming viewers may expect in coming years.

But before that was to happen, Spencer Christian, wearing a Starfleet uniform, joined Gates McFadden on the sickbay set. She brought her concertina with her and played it as she was introduced (to underscore her earlier anecdote). She showed some of the medical props used on the show and briefly revealed a 21st century antique hidden under the table. It was a dust buster. "So all of these things function to keep you very healthy and fit in the 24th century."

It was a very brief segment showing off the props without really showing any of them close-ups. They could have made much better use of their access to the set had they revealed more details (such as they did at the beginning of the show, when they opened on the bridge set).

THE FUTURE OF TELEVISION?

The entertainment chiefs of the three networks and Fox were introduced. It was pointed out that the three networks only divided up about sixty percent of the viewing audience these days instead of the ninety percent they held twenty years before. The chiefs were Peter Chernin, President of the Fox Broadcasting Company; Robert Iger, the President of ABC Entertainment; Warren Littlefield, the President of NBC Entertainment; and Jeff Sagansky, President of CBS Entertainment.

They discussed the impact of cable and, Jeff Sagansky expressed his opinion that the viewers had to be maxed out at 30 channels and wouldn't be interested in any more channels. They also didn't think that the network share would diminish. Robert Eiger suggested that the network share of the audience had pretty much leveled out at sixty percent. This was in 1992 before it was announced that by the year 2000 cable would have access to up to 500 channels. Television's transformation is happening very quickly. In 1992 they were expecting up to 100 channels. How many choices does a viewer really need, they wondered.

Peter Chernin of Fox said that in five years they had become very profitable, and he fully expected that a fifth and even a sixth network would come along. This prediction is starting to come to pass in 1994 with Warner

Dr. Crusher's office.
Photo c 1994 "Deep Focus"

Brothers and Paramount. "And I also don't agree that thirty channels maxes things out. I think we're going to see a hundred channels. I think there's a young generation which is going to know how to use them and I think we're going to see a lot more choices. And I think all it means is greater challenges to us as programmers."

THE QUESTION OF "R"-RATED TV

Jeff Sagansky was worried. "Right now, so much of the network business is that we schedule our shows, and by habit people know to turn on CBS on the Monday night lineup. What worries me is that technology will come along, and they'll be able to turn on those shows any time of the day. And—in which case—the thing that has sustained network television for forty years, that's going to be broken. And that could potentially undermine a lot of what's effective about our business."

The subject of Stephen Bochco came up. He had predicted "R" rated television for the networks, but the entertainment chiefs said they didn't think that would be a good idea. A year and a half later the Stephen Bochco series NYPD BLUE premiered on ABC, and it clearly is "R" rated television. So again the future arrived more quickly than the network entertainment chiefs believed it would in 1992. But in 1992 they didn't think that adding violence, nudity or profane language would be innovative. In 1994 the issue has changed. Many new shows will imitate NYPD BLUE.

Transporter pad.
Photo c 1994 "Deep Focus"

They will imitate the nudity and the profanity, while ignoring the quality of the writing. Of course, not everyone is as talented as Stephen Bochco, although many television writers and producers imagine they are.

With that the interview abruptly concluded.

"REALLY NEAT STUFF"

Following a commercial break Leonard Nimoy was shown saying "Good morning, America," to the viewing audience. This was followed by Joan Lunden's observation, Nimoy had directed some of the episodes of STAR TREK—THE NEXT GENERATION. This was incorrect, although Leonard's son Adam would soon report to the deck as a director of the series.

Once again, Joan was irresistably compelled to chirp about all the "really neat stuff around here. This is the Captain's Ready Room," she continued picking up the model of the Stargazer which was on that set. She remarked, it was the Captain's old ship. But then she garbled her facts stating that the Stargazer got "blown up in a battle with Maxia." Actually the Stargazer was presumed lost at the Battle of Maxia but was found intact years later.

As if to punish Joan for her faux pas, the screen suddenly went blank at the network level. After a few seconds the picture returned, but Charles Gibson and Joan Lunden were now standing on a darkened, only dimly illuminated set. Gibson stated, "We can see you. . . we just took a power hit. We are still on the air in the Captain's quarters here," and he then proceeded to reveal that in the final half hour of the show they'd be taking a look at cosmetic surgery. What that had to do with STAR TREK or any sort of futuristic slant remained as dim as their studio was at that moment. But they tried to salvage the linkage by revealing that an interview was upcoming with Michael Westmore, the head of make-up on STAR TREK.

The newscaster on GMA blamed the power outage on "dirty Klingons," but it was actually a result of the brutal storm which was ravaging Los Angeles County at the time.

IN THE ENGINEERING ROOM

The next interview was with LeVar Burton on the engineering set of STAR TREK—THE NEXT GENERATION. Burton was very ebullient, energetic and eager to talk about the show.

"The great thing about the concepts that we use here on STAR TREK are that they're actually based in fact. So this is—as I understand it—how this works," Burton began, standing in front of the engine room set. "Four floors above us there's a device that shoots a stream of hydrogen into this tube. Eight floors below us is the anti-matter injector. Matter and anti-matter meet here in the dilithium chamber and that gives us all the power we need to drive the warp engines."

This was another very brief interview such as the one with Gates McFadden. Following the segment on cosmetic surgery, a pre-taped sequence, host Charles Gibson returned introducing the segment on makeup artist Michael Westmore.

"We are now in the engine room of the Enterprise," Charles Gibson explained. "I don't suppose engines chug in the 24th century. Nonetheless these engines are whirring and puffing and ready to go to propel this ship through the bounds of space. We're going to go backstage; take you into the makeup room of STAR TREK.

"If you have ever watched this program," something one can safely assume Charles Gibson hadn't done up to that moment in his life, "you know how dependent STAR TREK—THE NEXT GENERATION is on the magic of a man named Michael Westmore. He is in charge of makeup on STAR TREK, and he has been working his magic for many years on the famous faces of Hollywood."

MAKEUP MAGIC

The show cut to a pre-taped interview with Westmore in his workshop showing many of the alien masks he created for the show. Westmore stated, "People think there's a lot of time to do this. Sometimes I only have

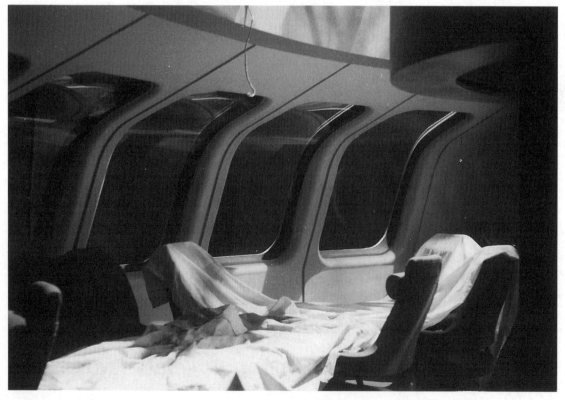

Obervation lounge from door-way to the bridge.
Photo c 1994 "Deep Focus"

weeks to put together a whole Klingon group—maybe twenty-five of them—and have them all ready. But our longest character we've ever had is LeVar Burton, when we had to turn him into a lizard. I had four artists working on him for six hours."

Westmore showed some of the alien masks and explained how they work. He made them with a range of possible expressions for each of the alien faces. "The furrowed brow or snarl or something ... so if you're doing a bad alien, little things like that can be done in a structure. You can either make lines go up or you can make lines go down, depending on the artificial expression that you want to create in your rubber.

"This is a process that really doesn't get tedious," Westmore explained. "And I'll tell you a good example. When I was doing RAGING BULL, I think it's the longest amount of time I've ever had to repeat a makeup—and

you're talking about putting eyelids and the nose on Deniro—I did it 113 times. There wasn't one time that I went to work where I said, gee, I wish I could stay in bed; I hate doing makeup."

While he was talking, he was making up an actor to be an alien, and he demonstrated little tricks of the trade.

Then came the final segment. The entire cast was brought back to talk—all except for Patrick Stewart.

"We are back once again with the cast of STAR TREK—THE NEXT GENERATION, which I believe has had about nine Emmys so far," Joan Lunden gushed. Back to speak were LeVar Burton, Marina Sirtis, Brent Spiner, Gates McFadden, Michael Dorn and Jonathan Frakes.

OBVIOUS QUESTIONS

"We were talking just before we came back from commercial about the fact

that this program—where we are this morning—is so different from all the other programs—where we've been all week long, which have been situation comedies. There's an audience there, and they go through these rehearsals, and then they shoot it with three cameras. It seems like this is almost more like a movie—the way it's shot," fumbled Lunden. Then she asked the age-old, shop-worn, question. How can they shoot scenes out of order and yet keep the story in their heads? How can they react properly? It never occurred to her that this is the purpose of the script. It maintains the continuity for the actor.

Marina Sirtis replied, "You read the script. That helps, if you know what's going on in the script." An obvious answer to a painfully obvious question.

The show is usually shot with one camera. Occasionally they use two—to get extra coverage. They put in long hours and shoot for seven days each episode.

Brent Spiner added, "The biggest difference—probably—is that people who do half hour shows have lives," referring to the fact that time off is rare for stars of a one-hour TV series.

"But you must enjoy working," Joan observed, "because one of the interesting things about this ensemble cast—here—is that you're doing things all together outside of this program. I know some of you are working on a play together. You did an album, right?" she asked Brent. "And you got some of them to sing backup?"

"We had one number where the four guys did the background vocals. And they were sensational! We did an Inkspots number, and we called ourselves the Sunspots. I know it's cliched, but we all actually like each other; I mean, except for John," he added jokingly.

FOOT IN MOUTH DISORDER

"I remember talking to you, LeVar, when you were first coming on the show. And you have to come in with this cast that's there. And you've got to work into the dynamics of it all. It's been fun?" Joan wondered aloud.

"It's been one of the best working experiences of my career," LeVar said. "I really love these people, and these people make it worth it—to come here every day and do this." Joan then asked about Gene Roddenberry, who had died just months before, and about Alex Haley, the author of ROOTS who had recently died as well.

Said LeVar, "I think we're all really lucky to have had the experience working with Gene. Alex—again, another giant in his field—who has passed... Both men of tremendous vision... And it's nice that we're able to honor their memory."

Joan thanked them all for being there. As they broke away for a commercial, Michael Dorn made a joke that he probably believed would not be picked up by the micro-phone and broadcast over the air. He said, "You know Paul Bunyon died. He was a giant in his field."

Say what? Talk about inappropriate humor. While there's nothing off-color about the remark, coming on the heels of a discussion about the passing of Gene Roddenberry and Alex Haley; it had to sound, well, stupid at best.

Following the commercial break, Joan Lunden, Charles Gibson and Spencer Christian were seen standing on the transporter pad.

"And our thanks to everyone here at STAR TREK—THE NEXT GENERATION," said Joan as GOOD MORNING AMERICA signed off for February 13, 1992. And after Charles Gibson did a promo for the next day's show, Spencer Christian said, "So let's beam out of here. From all of us at GOOD MORNING AMERICA—have a cosmic day!" And with that the three dematerialized, complete with appropriate sound effects.

ABSENT WITHOUT LEAVE

So that was the end, and yet it wasn't the end. What did happen to Patrick Stewart? Ordinarily, when the entire cast—minus one—appears on a show, they say something about the absent individual even if it's nothing more than a lame joke. But no one said anything about Patrick. It was clearly a deliberate omition without mentioning him. But why?

I had my answer about a month later in the April 1992 issue of SPY magazine. On page 20, in the column "Naked City," was the following lead item: "Just how does a celebrity draw the line between infotainment, good sportsmanship and unseemly shtick? One morning recently on GOOD MORNING AMERICA, Patrick Stewart, who plays Captain Picard on the syndicated TV show STAR TREK—THE NEXT GENERATION, was about to be interviewed. As Stewart awaited his moment, he noticed that Spencer Christian, GMA's weatherman, was dressed in a STAR TREK getup. Stewart, perhaps all too keenly aware that he risks the camp fate of William Shatner, stalked out of the studio, enraged. As it happened, the botched segment was on the same morning as an on-air discussion among the four men who control TV programming in America—Bob Iger from ABC, Warren Littlefield from NBC, Jeff Sagansky from CBS and Peter Chernin from Fox—and they evidently all witnessed Stewart's mad scene. 'So,' one of the network presidents said with a smile to a fellow network president, 'we're agreed—nobody will give Patrick Stewart any more work?' "

Whether the remark was said in jest or not, having the most powerful men in television see an actor get his knickers in a knot over something that was really very trivialcould not have enhanced Patrick Stewart's reputation. Walking off a set means that somebody broke their word, and in television walking off a set often costs somebody money. As it turned out, the rest of the cast was still there to be interviewed. But Paramount had, no doubt, promised that everyone would participate.

A PUBLIC APOLOGY

Of course, there exist doubts as to the accuracy of the above news item; but Patrick Stewart confirmed it himself in the July 31, 1992 issue of TV GUIDE, just five months after the incident occurred. We'll never know exactly how much trouble he made for himself by his actions. But he was more than willing to express public regret, when the interviewer for TV GUIDE asked Stewart about walking off the set of GOOD MORNING AMERICA.

Said Stewart, who confirmed the incident, "Yes. They were broadcasting from the NEXT GENERATION set, and the weatherman was dressed in a Star Fleet uniform. I thought that it was disrespectful. They were doing shtick in our costumes, and I thought it was demeaning to the show. I know I sound pompous, and I don't give a damn. Nevertheless, I should not have done what I did. I regret it."

The actor went on to state, "I'm at my least diplomatic, when there's a lack of respect. And I'm not speaking only of me, but when I see anyone or any group of people being treated disrespectfully. That's when I'm inclined to lose it."

So what was said after that episode of GOOD MORNING AMERICA was aired, was much more interesting than whatever was said on the episode itself. The morning spent on the set of STAR TREK—THE NEXT GENERATION was two hours of missed opportunities. Like many shows—done on the sets of other films and TV series—the interviews were superficial and the information was

skimpy. No doubt, Paramount put some restrictions on what could be done and shown; but it would have been much more interesting to have had the camera roam freely through the sets. It may have given an impression of exactly how they are linked and what actually goes on behind the sets themselves. In view of GOOD MORNING AMERICA'S bumbling attempt, none of the magic would have been worn off..

BEHIND THE SCENES

Because GMA aired live on the east coast, it was broadcasted from Los Angeles at 4 to 6 AM. This would have been before STAR TREK—THE NEXT GENERATION would have begun filming for the day. Why not show the preparations which go on to prepare for filming, such as dressing a set, arranging the lights, and other things which are just rarely seen by the mass television audience? There were any number of possi-

bilities, all of which would have been more interesting than yet another segment on cosmetic surgery in the '90s.

Whenever a TV crew is allowed access to a film set, they seldom seem to know what to do or where to begin. This results in a boring sameness to all of these behind-the-scenes specials. All one need do is send an advance team one week before the filming is to be done. And after several days there, they'll have ferreted out the interesting aspects of the production to be examined. You can't just show up the night before and expect to have a lot of great ideas for shooting and interviewing the next day. But that's the nature—and the drawback—of live television. It tends to be homogeniously unimaginative. The interviews with the network presidents, alone (which could have been done any morning on the show), had any substance or interest to sustain them. It's just too bad; the concept didn't spill over into the other interviews done that morning. But, apparently, there's a rule on daytime TV: actor interviews must be vacuous.

One would have thought—when broadcasting live from the set of a popular science fiction series—an imaginative quality to the proceedings would have been a stringent requirement. Instead, we are victimized by the usual babble. One need not wait in line for tickets to Short Attention Span Theatre; it's on the airwaves and coming at your television everyday for free.

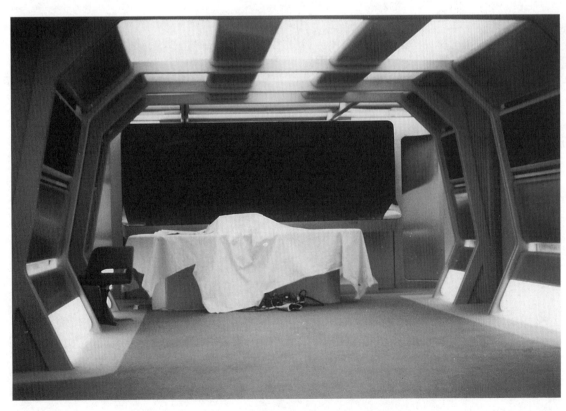

Main engineering.
Photo c 1994
"Deep Focus"

Next Generation comic book cover by Jerome Moore.

DRAWING STAR TREK COMIC BOOKS: AN INTERVIEW WITH JEROME MOORE AND JASON PALMER

The various versions of STAR TREK have spawned a variety of tie-in items, and some of the most interesting ones have been the comic books. These visually relate the all new adventures of the Enterprise and Deep Space Nine. Two artists, long associated with these comics, are also friends of mine and long-time STAR TREK fans.

Jerome Moore and Jason Palmer have done a lot of professional comic book work in recent years. But the art which fans would most quickly recognize are their covers for various STAR TREK comics. They know each other well; but they have only collaborated a few times, although they have both drawn covers for the same title on an alternating basis.

Jerome's first professional STAR TREK comic art was done about the time DC had canceled the title. DC brought it back on a trial basis in 1986.

"I did two or three covers," said Jerome. "And then I did the last issue, which was #56, which I penciled and inked on my own. By that time STAR TREK [the comic book] was already canceled because Paramount didn't like a lot of the things that DC was doing. They did like my artwork, but I just came along too late.

"I knew that STAR TREK — as a comic book — was going to start up again because the movie, THE VOYAGE HOME, was doing very well. So I knew that DC would start publishing it again. Bob Greenberger, the editor, said that Paramount really liked what I had done on that last cover. He was considering me for actually doing the interiors of the book. But at the time I was doing something else so [instead] he considered me for doing the covers for both magazines."

Jerome stated that at first he wasn't much of a fan of THE NEXT GENERATION. "The show took awhile to grow on me. I was basically a Classic [Trek] fan, so I jumped at the chance [to draw for the regular STAR TREK comic] and for the first seven issues I did regular covers for it, and Paramount really liked it a

lot. I got to go on the set and meet most of the actors and that was in '87. I've been [doing the covers] off and on ever since.

"Once I found out that Malibu was going to be doing DS9, I was asked to do the first issue's cover, along with Jason Palmer, but he didn't get around to working on it. I've gotten a name for myself doing STAR TREK covers now," Jerome explained. "I've been in the business a long time - about ten or eleven years - but when I really made my mark, it was doing the STAR TREK covers.

"I've actually been doing those things since I was a kid - drawing my own STAR TREK strips - so it was almost like a dream come true doing STAR TREK." None of his amateur work has ever been published, though. "I was never really in to fanzines when I was coming up. I'd buy comics and I went to an occasional convention, but I was never seriously into it. I did my own stuff and sold it to my friends, but I

never went into fanzines. And don't ask because I'm never going to dig that stuff up. I pretty much hide all my old artwork."

Jerome described the approach he takes to doing a cover, "For NEXT GENERATION it's a lot easier because there's more reference available. For Classic [Trek], they come out with a film every few years and then STARLOG will publish a [tie-in] magazine so you can get most of your reference from that. DC has pretty much stayed away from doing the old Classic series from TV, because they feel that all that material has been pretty well mined by Gold Key and [in] the TV series which ran for three years. So they don't want to go with that material. They want to stay with the modern era - the classic movie era - so the [available] reference there is a little bit harder. But with THE NEXT GENERATION you get the four magazines a year from STARLOG, so that's a little easier so far as reference goes."

Next Generation comic book cover by Jason Palmer and Jerome Moore.

REALISM VERSUS EXAGGERATION

"What I do is draw from the reference," said Jerome, "using mostly photographs, because what I mostly do is portraiture, similar to what Keith Birdsong does on the novels." But unlike the way the characters had previously been drawn in the comic books, Jerome goes for a realistic look. This is opposed to an exaggerated comic book version - such as Marvel and D.C. did - familiar to fans prior to Jerome's work on the titles.

"They had everything translated into what Spock would look like as a comic book character. Even the first NEXT GENERATION mini-series is that way. They had the characters so that they could appeal to a wider audience of comic book fans. They had them structured so that the anatomy was such that you could see the muscles through Picard's uniform, which was ridiculous to me. Likenesses weren't really that key; it wasn't really stressed. But with me I wanted to go more towards movie poster design, inspired by like what Drew Struzan does. He's done STAR WARS posters, Indiana Jones and book jacket work. So I had more of an influence where I'm going to nail the likenesses. That's what people are going to buy it for. That's going to jump out at you on the stands.

"I don't want to compete with Spider-Man and X-Men where the action is just over the top, and I don't think STAR TREK should try to compete with them," Jerome added. "I wanted to go the other way and do things a little bit more subtle that will draw you in. You'll walk by the comic book rack and you'll look and see all the stuff just glaring at you and screaming for attention, and STAR TREK will stand out on its own by doing something totally different."

WHAT MAKES A GOOD COVER?

This is how he conceives a cover; Jerome revealed that he gets a script and then reads the entire script. "It's sort of like doing a book report back in school where you'd have to read a book and get the main theme of it; the main thrust of what the author is telling you. Then I pick whatever key scene I think is most interesting, and I try to portray that on the cover.

"The cover is supposed to sell the book. That's the first thing that the reader is going to see. So I've got to pretty much play up certain angles. Maybe I'll go over the top on certain action. Say there's a phaser battle or some kind of a shocking ending where Spock finds out that somebody just died - I'll play that up on the cover - even if it's goosing it just a little bit. Or maybe it's not entirely what's depicted inside the book, just to get the attention. That's what the cover's supposed to do. It's just a fancy wrapper. So I do a sketch of that, and then I send it back to DC, and they send it to Paramount.

"That's the one frustrating angle about working on these books - all the red tape involved. You have to get all the approval from Paramount. First you have to get it past your editor. Then it has to be checked by Paramount, so there's a lot of checks and balances in it. After I get approval, then I work up the final version," Jerome explained.

For the most Part Jerome has had little trouble getting his cover art approved. "Because I concentrate on the likenesses, I don't make too many waves. But one time I did a cover, and I stuck Kirstie Alley's likeness on the character called R.J. Blaze. She was created by Peter David and it was like an on-going character that was created by the writer and injected into the STAR TREK universe. But she doesn't really belong in there. Sometimes it's really hard for a writer to get up for a book, unless he can inject his own creativity," Jerome observed.

ARTISTIC DIFFERENCES

"So Peter David created this character R.J. Blaze who was an officer from the Federation, and she was pretty much assigned to bird-dog Kirk, because Kirk had always gone against the Prime Directive - here and there - and bent certain rules. She was supposed to keep an eye on him. So I designed her, and she was a very sexy looking young woman; the kind who would attract Kirk's eye. She was a protocol officer, and I designed her to look like Kirstie Alley, and I thought I could get away with it. I don't really like that fact, that she was replaced by Robin Curtis [as Saavik in the movies]. There was a lot of stuff that went into that, but she really caught my attention as a character, and I thought she was the ideal actress to play Saavik. I tried to get away with that and actually Paramount didn't catch it. Somebody at D.C. caught it after Paramount had already

approved it. I almost got away with it, but not quite. So that one I had to change."

Jerome also had to make a couple of changes on the first DEEP SPACE NINE cover for Malibu.

"They want Dax pretty much to remain not really sexual; they don't want her to portray any kind of sexuality. She's a beautiful woman, but I had her hair in a ponytail draped over her shoulder on the first issue's cover, and they said, 'We don't want any feminine flourish in her hair.' They want Dax to be an alluring character but not over the top sexually. I didn't think that was really over the top, so I don't always agree with their changes. Also I had Major Kira holding her Bajoran weapon, her phaser, and it wasn't anything overtly violent in context; she was just brandishing it." But Paramount didn't want to see that.

"Sometimes they'll be arbitrary about certain things just to maintain Gene Roddenberry's

Next Generation comic book cover by Jerome Moore.

image of STAR TREK being this peaceful non-George Lucas STAR WARS type of universe. Now and then, I come across where Paramount draws the line. I also got some flack for not including Bashir, but I wanted to keep the images as simple as I could without cramming too many in there; you've got eight characters on that show. Originally the sketch started with just four and I added Dax and O'Brien."

LIFELONG STAR TREK FANS

Jason Palmer is another artist who draws covers for STAR TREK comics and other related products. Like Jerome, Jason is also interested in the series beyond the requirements of the job.

"Jerome and I have been fans all our lives so that helps as far as being accurate artists. We know so much about it, we know how to put little extra things in it that we think the fans would appreciate."

But Jerome observed that among some professionals there's a stigma attached if you know "too much" about a subject as though one is leaning towards William Shatner's reference to "Get a life." Also, although Paramount used to provide artists with reference, Jerome explained that a few years ago the word came down that the artists weren't supposed to contact Paramount directly any more.

"This happened when Gene Roddenberry was still alive," Jerome recalled," and Richard Arnold was still the research consultant. I used to go around that and just contact them directly anyway, but something happened where there was so much stuff going on with all the novels and the comic books that they got to a point where they said they want to streamline everything and keep everything in the same continuity and get rid of all the 'garbage' that was going on. So they were cracking the whip and saying, 'okay, this is going to be set up where you're going to have to contact Richard Arnold directly for all approval and we'll deal only with the licensees,' which meant DC at the time as well as Malibu now. So you got your reference through DC."

But it also depended on the client, Jason Palmer added. "We've had some editors who are very good about providing reference, whereas others say they can never find anything. But you find out later they did have it. It just depends on how into it that editor is. I've also worked on STAR TREK projects that had nothing to do with the comics, and they don't have the first clue how to get reference."

GETTING THE DETAILS RIGHT

Jerome explained, it is easier, when you're working on an adaptation of a film, because it's an encapsulated saga where there is specific reference for specific story scenes, whereas STAR TREK is a more complicated on-going series. "I almost worked on a film adaptation, and it's a lot of headaches but they give you all the reference and you can go down to the studio and go through the slides and whatnot. So that's a different situation than what we're doing."

Bob Greenberger, a DC editor, also had an affiliation with STARLOG magazine and so would be able to help get good reference for the STAR TREK comic books. But beyond that, since he's a fan of the show, whenever he sees something on the newsstand, Jerome buys it and therefore has his own reference material on hand.

"And we borrow from each other," Jason stated. "It's like a couple of sisters going through each other's closets for clothes. We each did a cover for the adaptation of STAR TREK VI, and we got plenty of reference, but we didn't know who was who [among the new charac-ters, since they hadn't yet seen the film itself]. There was one character that Kirk had to fight in the prison. I figured he was the big savage guy that was described as the person that Iman turned into. So I did the painting where they're kind of melding into each other, and it turns out that it was somebody else, because they never showed the beast that she turned into. So we're watching the movie, and that character was on screen and off again, and it turned out that she turned into something else. So you don't know until you see the movie.

"Also I thought that the grandfather of Worf was going to have a much more significant part, so I made him very big on the cover. And he was hardly in it at all. And then General Chang was the main bad guy, and I had him real small because I just didn't know who was who. Sometimes you don't know how everything relates, and it gets real frustrating."

BREAKING IN

Jason Palmer's first professional STAR TREK artwork was the cover for the trade paperback THE BEST OF STAR TREK which reprinted some of the DC comic book stories.

"Jerome got me into the business," Jason explained. "We were friends for a long time, but I didn't get into it early. I only pursued art when I was twenty-two, and then it took me about four or five years before I was good enough. And along the way, every once in awhile Jerome would say, 'Try coloring this, and I'll see if I can get you the job.' And I'd always get carried away and try to make this big spectacular deal about it and always bit off too much. I wasn't ready for that. Finally he got me some work with Innovation doing LOST IN SPACE, and then - based on that work - I met Bob [Greenberger] through Jerome, and he offered me a cover. And ever since then, I've been doing trade paperbacks. Then Jerome

Cover for The Next Generation #52 by Jason Palmer and Jerome Moore.

wanted to cut back at a crucial shuffling point with the editorial staff, so I took over [the covers] of THE NEXT GENERATION. And that led to a lot of other STAR TREK work outside of comics."

Jerome was getting tired of doing so many STAR TREK covers all the time, and so D.C. allowed him to choose his successor. "Jason took over, and now that I'm trying to get back in, he won't let me," he said jokingly.

"We're going to try swapping art," said Jason, "where I'll do Classic for awhile, and then he'll do NEXT GENERATION, and go back and forth and kind of keep it fresh for us."

"Out of all of them," Jerome stated, "although I still love Classic Trek, NEXT GENERATION has taken the lead of what I like to do. DS9 has not grown on me yet, so I don't enjoy doing too much with DEEP SPACE NINE. Malibu had a great start with that first issue. It got a lot of attention. They did it really well. I think

their first issue was the best debut for a STAR TREK title in comics that was ever done. All the way through the quality was up."

INSIDE DEEP SPACE NINE

Regarding his approach to doing the cover of Malibu's DEEP SPACE NINE #1, Jerome explained, "The cover was a combination of a painting style plus the standard black and white, which is what I usually do. They did a blueline on that. Gold Key did paintings and they did photo covers, but they didn't really meld the two. Malibu pretty much covered all the bases. They did a photo cover, a blue line which was a painting and they really had a very good jumping off point. It remains to be seen whether or not they're going to be able to maintain any kind of quality there. I'm still doing an occasional cover for them. I've done three already, and inked one and hope to do some more for them.

But right now DS9 is not really my favorite to do."

Regarding the characters on this new version of STAR TREK, Jerome has some specific observations relating to the series itself.

"I like Sisko, but he has a lot of potential that's not being tapped yet. Odo is interesting. He's like the Data type - the Spock type character that has a lot of secrets behind him that you want to explore. I like Kira, mainly because she's more or less a defacto Ensign Ro. It's just the dark nature of it, like being trapped on that station and the religious undertones of the Bajorans is what I think is hamstringing it. I prefer the whole STAR TREK credo of going out where no man has gone before."

"Instead of to boldly sit where no one has sat before," Jason observed.

"I've heard someone say that it's like HOTEL in space," Jerome continued. "We're not really getting to see too much of the Gamma Quadrant, but it's still young, so you have to give it a chance."

ANOTHER NEW STAR TREK

On the subject of the proposed new STAR TREK television series, Jerome stated, "I'm interested in seeing what's going to happen with STAR TREK VOYAGER. Other than the fact that it sounds a little bit like LOST IN SPACE—they're out there pretty much trying to find their way back. But to be out there on the edge, exploring."

"I thought they should have gone the other way," Jason suggested. "What would have been great was if they had a series that was about Starfleet and not one specific crew of seven members that we see over and over again. It's such a well-defined universe. I think the fun would have been exploring little niches; catching up with characters that we've seen in previous movies or episodes and seeing what they're doing now. I think that would have been a lot of fun to explore. I don't know what restraints would keep them from doing something like that. I just thought it would be fun to see what life is like on the [USS] Hood for awhile, and then go with the Intrepid and then go back to Starfleet Command. Bounce around; have an anthology series. It would be nice to have that.

"I was talking to my uncle, who's a huge STAR TREK fan; he kind of started me on it, and he said, 'What a shame we're not going to have an Enterprise,' except for the movies. We'll have two series and no Enterprise around. So I think people are going to miss that."

Jerome pointed out that STAR TREK started out being just a story about one ship, and they pretty much carried that over into THE NEXT GENERATION. "So that would be an interesting idea to see because the STAR TREK universe is so broad that you want to explore all these different things. They'll visit a certain planet and stop there, and you'll wonder, 'well what happened with these people?'

THE WORLD OF STAR TREK

"A friend of mine over at Hanna-Barbera had the same idea. He said, 'Since we've gotten away from the Enterprise being the sole focus of the STAR TREK series, wouldn't it be cool just to bounce around, like a STAR TREK chronicles sort of thing.' You'd have one episode in the past in Starfleet, maybe even before Kirk got there. Then in the next episode you could jump out to the core planets on the rim somewhere defending against Romulan space or Klingon space. And to link them all you'd hire a certain group of actors for one episode, and maybe one would take a ship out to a certain location, and then the next episode would follow that individual. And then from there you'd meet a new group of characters."

Next Generation comic book cover by Jerome Moore.

"Or you could take established characters," Jason added. "You could find out what happened to Benjamin Maxwell ["The Wounded"] or Wesley Crusher or Thomas Riker ["Second Chances"]. There's so many possibilities. I think they're doing the opposite by sticking the VOYAGER out into a completely uncharted realm of space."

It seems as though Paramount is trying to do with VOYAGER what it did with STAR TREK when everything was new; the only way to do that, now, is to go to a part of the galaxy which is unexplored and which has had no previous contact with the Federation.

"NEXT GEN has done the same thing," Jerome suggested. "When they first got out of the gate they wanted to stay so far away from what was already established in the original TREK: 'All right! We've gone out further than they have, and our mission is longer and we're going to meet more aliens.'

And they just kept on adding more and more aliens, all of them humanoid, and I think that gets too unwieldy."

It would be interesting to go back and see more of what's already been established, which is what Jerome wishes they would at least do with the comic book. "There's all this stuff going on with little tag lines they'll drop about a certain race or a certain conference that happened or a treaty in THE NEXT GENERATION. Picard mentioned the Treaty of Algernon that said something about how the Federation could not develop cloak technology, which answered a lot of the fans' questions. They answered another question why can't Picard have a romance with Beverly Crusher on the ship. [see "Lessons."] They had an episode why that wouldn't work."

UNTOLD TALES OF STAR TREK

Jerome feels that the comic books establish the perfect opportunity to explore ideas like that, and

he cites the Chris Claremont graphic novel "Debt Of Honor" as a perfect example. It was done so well, because Chris Claremont was so diligent in studying the series and exploring aspects of the continuity.

"Yes," Jason agreed, "not only did he study the whole series but he studied the movies and NEXT GENERATION and did backwards references from NEXT GENERATION with Chateau Picard," which is the name on a bottle of wine in the very last scene of the graphic novel.

"I only wish that Paramount would not be that restrictive about it," Jerome observed, "because they didn't want sequels done to the series. They had an edict, that they made known early on, in so far as the comic book people [were concerned], that they didn't want any sequels to episodes that we've already seen on TV. Now and then they've gotten away with it, but for the most part, when

Roddenberry was there he didn't want that."

Even now a comic book story will sometimes carry a disclaimer, such as in a recent Borg/Mirror, Mirror type storyline in issues 47-50 of THE NEXT GENERATION. "They had to come out and say that this is a parallel universe STAR TREK," Jason stated. "They had to disclaim that it was actual STAR TREK. It was like it wasn't a real STAR TREK story."

The covers of the issues of NEXT GENERATION which Jason Palmer was illustrating at the time were for a storyline which was based on a reference Picard made in the episode "Allegiance." He made this reference visiting the planet Chalnoth - twelve years before - when he was on the Stargazer. "They did a flashback story: when he did visit Chalnoth and met that race. So it's fun for me; because I get to do a cover with the Stargazer, Picard with hair and Jack Crusher."

A UNIVERSE OF POSSIBILITIES

"I think some of the better stories are done that way," Jerome agreed. "John deLancie did the first STAR TREK—THE NEXT GENERATION annual for D.C. called "The Gift." He did the whole scene which we later saw in 'Tapestry' [the sixth season TNG episode] where Picard confronted those Nausicaans and gets stabbed. When I saw it in 'Tapestry' it seemed like, 'Are they reading our stuff and ripping us off?' That occasionally happens where the comics have a good idea and it can't be done, because Paramount says they're already doing that. Michael Jan Friedman, the writer of THE NEXT GENERA-TION, had come up with an idea for a Romulan who defected from the Romulan Empire and he couldn't do it because Paramount already was. Several times that has happened."

Jason Palmer pointed out that the seventh season episode "Parallels" drew one aspect from a comic book story. THE NEXT GENERATION comic book had previously done a story in which the Borg had destroyed the Federation in a parallel universe.

Jerome pointed out that Paramount takes the stance that they're the official STAR TREK, "And it gets frustrating - now and then - when you want to tell good STAR TREK stories. But you're restricted. And whenever you do come up with a real good idea, they've already got that idea. I would like the comic books to stick a little bit closer to the series and the films, and do an episode that actually appears in-between, like a bridge between two episodes. But the comic book depends on what Paramount will allow. The tremendous faux pas in STAR TREK II - one of my favorite episodes - is that Khan never really met Chekov; but he says he has. Why couldn't the comic book do a flashback which goes back to the first season of the first

Next Generation comic book cover by Jerome Moore.

Cover for Deep Space Nine #3 by Jerome Moore.

series and show that maybe Chekov was below decks?"

THE JASON PALMER APPROACH

Jason explained how he arrives at the image he chooses for the cover paintings he does.

"One thing I find with designs is that either they come very easy—somebody can tell me over the phone what it is—or they'll send me a script, and I'll read it and immediately get an idea. And that's great, and that's what it winds up being." But, if he doesn't get the idea immediately, he has to work at it. "You have to always go back to your basics if there's a problem. In fact, just recently I was working with Steve Rude; I'll just go over, and we'll both just work out of his place. It's just nice having another artist there, because I usually work alone. Steve will make sure that I get the stuff done. That I need, because he

says, 'You're a good artist but you've got to get your designs down better.' Because I don't always do that. I work out a lot of the design elements as I'm actually painting the cover, and that's just a backwards way of doing it.

"I've realized that all the great artists, especially with a painting, always get their values, their design elements and their proportions really straightened out ahead of time. It's so easy to go back to your old bad habits, and it's good to have someone there to remind you. If you look at Frazetta or Drew Struzan or Steve Rude you see the values all worked out. The design works without having to recognize the elements."

WITH A GOAL IN MIND

Jerome added his own observations on artistic basics and creating a piece of art. "Once you find your style, everything else falls into place. Originally, I had decided that I wanted

to do everything in a book jacket style, so I've already got my design. After that, it's pretty much that I want to stick as close to the series - either feature films or the TV series - as far as the look of it. I don't want to translate it into comic book action, as I said before. I don't want to do the over the top violence." And no word balloons. "I hate cover copy. I want everything to be as panoramic a view as I can get. I had a cover where I did Guinan in Ten Forward and there's a Klingon battle going on around her. The whole crew had been transmuted into Klingons, and cover copy would have messed that whole idea up. It was nothing but mayhem all over the place.

"But for the most part - for the feature film classic material - I'll go for a movie type flavor. A lot of the action is very subtle. I did one cover where the ship is supposed to be leaving Earth orbit, and the typical comic book way of doing that is a very boring image. But I wanted to go for something more like the film, so I had the ship just sitting there in space - no speed lines - and the rest of it, you have to fill in the gaps with your mind. The same thing with NEXT GENERATION, I'll do Picard talking to somebody - and you can't just get the likeness down - you have to do the body language. Picard stands a certain way. Riker stands a certain way.

"There was one episode, where Riker was kidnapped, and they were doing something with his mind. And he kept on believing that he was on the ship doing a play." This was the sixth season episode, "Frame Of Mind," which included some striking imagery of scenes shattering and breaking up. "That special effect - of him shattering - just stuck in my mind. And I used that as inspiration for the cover to DEEP SPACE NINE #3, where Odo is supposed to solve a murder mystery, and I've got all these puzzle pieces floating around him. The whole idea is that the murder mystery is the puzzle that he has to solve, and the faces of the suspects are on the tiles of the puzzle pieces floating around him. And in the back there's this overall image of the Cardassian that was murdered. His image is actually the puzzle, and it's shattering."

MEETING OF THE MINDS

Jason explained that he starts out laying the colors down with a wash and airbrush, and then he adds detail. That is how he paints. "I detail it with a brush and prisma colored pencils.

"When I'm designing something like this," Jason added, "dealing with the Chalnoths - that I mentioned before - I try to get the feel. The Chalnoth is a lion-like character, and in STAR TREK there's a certain look to how ships are. I wanted something that looked a bit savage - and yet elegant, like a cat. So it had to fit in with STAR TREK. And [the ship] had to fit in with the Chalnoth.

For instance, if you were designing a ship for the STAR WARS universe, the engine would be more integral to the body of the ship. Whereas in STAR TREK, there's more to do with the warp technology with the twin engines. So I came up with a [Chalnoth] ship that has these twin engines. You always have to think in terms of being in the STAR TREK universe."

On the covers which Jason has done using straight linework - as opposed to paintings - he feels that Jerome has been the best inker over his work. "We think a lot alike - as far as what a cover should be and how things should look. It's always nice, because - sometimes - I'll take an idea, and once I've started it, he knows that he can take it a little farther and push it, until it becomes even better."

Jason described a Dixon Hill cover on the NEXT GENERATION comic book which was originally Jerome's idea for the scene. Jerome simplified what Jason did with it.

And the final result was quite impressive.

"Jerome has a very painterly style with his inking," Jason observed. "He uses many different textures. He uses the roughness of the page and picks it up with the China Marker, and that gives one texture. He does the splatter. And then he puts white over that for another texture. It keeps it very exciting; it's not all uniform."

While every artist who has worked on the STAR TREK comics over the years has not been as interested in the subject as Jerome Moore and Jason Palmer, you can tell - when an artist truly cares about the subject they are illustrating - because there is an underlying excitement and a grasp of the imaginative subtext of the material. It shows through in the final product. Truly, that sets the STAR TREK art of these two artists apart from their comic book contemporaries.

Michael Dorn at the Technical Emmys presentation.
Photo c 1994 Albert L. Ortega

THE MOVIE INFLUENCES OF STAR TREK—THE NEXT GENERATION

Good ideas for a story comes from somewhere. Sometimes, a story is "inspired" by someone else's motion picture.

Everything is influenced by something, as the old saying goes, but in television those influences tend to be more readily traced. In some cases the writers and producers will, no doubt, claim that this is just a "coincidence," but sometimes one can stretch that explanation a bit too far. These days such influences are referred to as an "homage."

"The Galileo Seven," one of the episodes of the original STAR TREK, was no more than a thinly disguised rewrite of the Robert Aldrich film FLIGHT OF THE PHOENIX which starred Jimmy Stewart, Richard Attenborough, Peter Finch, Ernest Borgnine, and George Kennedy. That earlier film told the tale of a plane crew who crash in an Arabian desert and must somehow overcome their differences to survive. For the most part, though, Classic Trek didn't rely on films for inspiration.

The same cannot be said of STAR TREK—THE NEXT GENERATION where several episodes have their genesis in popular film plots (just as some episode titles from the original series came from Shakespearean plays, e.g. "Dagger of the Mind," "Conscience of the King," "All Our Yesterdays" and "By Any Other Name").

Initially, STAR TREK—THE NEXT GENERATION depended more on rewrites of Classic Trek episodes, when inspiration failed to strike, though one episode title in the first season, "We'll Always Have Paris," is a clear CASABLANCA reference. The line derives from one given by Ingrid Bergman's character Ilsa to Humphrey Bogart's Rick Blain. Ilsa fell in love with Rick, after believing that her husband was killed by the Germans, and she and Rick spent many happy hours together in Paris before the city was taken over by the Nazis. Years later in Casablanca, Ilsa runs across Rick and discovers that her loyalties are divided. Her husband, played by Paul Henried, is an important man in the underground fighting against the Nazis. She finds she cannot abandon him, and so tries to assure Rick that her memory of their love affair in Paris will always remain (i.e., we can't be together now, but we'll always have our memories of Paris).

In the NEXT GENERATION episode "We'll Always Have Paris," Picard's old flame Jenice (Michelle Phillips of the pop group The Mamas and the Papas) appears on shipboard bringing Picard's unresolved feelings to the surface. In a twist on the original, this time he left her waiting while he shipped out. Instead of the song "As Time Goes By," Jenice's husband Paul is working on time experiments which have gone awry. However, Jenice remains faithful to her man, unlike Ilsa who decided to let Rick do the thinking for the both of them.

The NEXT GENERATION episode, which never really generates any romantic chemistry between the leads, isn't the classic romance that CASABLANCA was, and its dialogue could have used quite a bit more polish. The matte painting shown in a holodeck sequence is an unsatisfactory replacement for getting a look at what a 24th century Paris might be like, but that's just one of many unsatisfactory elements in this tired rehash of clichés.

POINTS OF VIEW

Another classic movie which influenced a NEXT GENERATION episode is "A Matter of Perspective," which drew on Akira Kurosawa's classic RASHOMON for inspiration. The original film dealt with a small group of men in a rainstorm who rehash a recent trial in an effort to get at the truth. Each person describes the events quite differently, and each makes himself or herself the hero of their narrative.

A bandit brags about how clever he was to fool a man by tying him up and ravishing his wife. She then insists that the bandit

must kill her husband. So ensues a prolonged and dazzling sword fight which ends with the husband's death.

The wife's story is that she was raped, and that her husband regarded her with only hatred, so she killed him - while in a daze - with a dagger.

A medium summons the husband's spirit from hell. His version is that after raping his wife, she insisted that the bandit kill the husband, which the bandit refused to do.

A Next Generation Celebration   **49**

Discovering that his wife is unworthy, the husband uses his dagger to kill himself.

A woodcutter, who happened to see the incident, reports that after the rape the wife insisted that one of them must die, and then she would commit suicide. The men don't wish to fight, until she taunts them into it. Instead of being great swordsmen, both men are inept and cowardly adversaries, until the bandit finally gains the upper hand. The woodcutter's story might seem convincing until it is revealed that he omitted the fact that he stole the dagger from the murder scene to pawn it. The truth becomes ultimately unknowable, because no one can be totally objective. The subjective viewpoints color what is seen.

In "A Matter of Perspective," Riker is accused of murdering Dr. Nel Apgar (Mark Margolis) who dies in an explosion aboard a space station. Seconds earlier Riker had beamed aboard the Enterprise from the station. The holodeck is used to recreate what actually happened. Each person relates the events in ways that favor them. Riker reports that Manua Apgar (Gina Hecht) flirted with him, but he rejected her. Meanwhile, she reports it the other way around. A third recreation shows that Riker didn't have a motivation to murder Nel Apgar, but it shows that Apgar had intended to murder Riker. Apgar wanted to keep Riker from reporting his breakthrough to the Federation. Apgar hoped to develop his discovery into a weapon. Riker beamed out during an experiment which defected the weapon's beam, killing Apgar in the process. This final version is accepted as the truth by Inspector Krag (Craig Richard Nelson) leaving nothing for contemplation at this routine episode's end.

VASH AND Q

Not all movie-influenced episodes lift their entire plots from old films. Some, such as "Q-Pid" are simply inspired by them. Perhaps, influenced by the dull Kevin Costner version of ROBIN HOOD which proved to be a huge box office hit, John deLancie's Q plops the Enterprise crew into a standard Robin Hood plot. This episode is most memorable, and quotable, for the moment when Worf examines his ludicrous get-up and intones one in a most querulous tone: "I am not a merry man!"

That episode is a follow-up to "Captain's Holiday" which took such adventures as ROMANCING THE STONE and RAIDERS OF THE LOST ARK for inspiration. Picard becomes involved with Vash (Jennifer Hetrick) in a plot revolving around the mechanizations of several groups to retrieve a valuable archeological artifact, the Tox Uthat. It is believed - like the ark of the covenant - to be a super weapon. United in purpose, Picard and Vash begin to have romantic feelings for each other.

In "Q-Pid," Q discovers that Picard neglected to mention anything about Vash to his crew; nor has Picard admitted his feelings to her. So Q arranges a Robin Hood scenario in which Picard is Robin and Vash is captive, soon-to-be-executed Maid Marion. Q wants to see if Picard will risk his men to rescue her.

Neither episode is a carbon copy of their inspiration. Rather, they are playful examinations of the clichés that they employ. Vash's unpredictability helps keep the episode from being too true to the form of the original. Though she can be aggravating, one sees the qualities of intelligence and independence that Picard admires in her. She is a strong-minded and strong-willed woman who would make a deal with the devil to get her ends, and is one of the more dynamic female characters that the Trek universe has ever presented.

MINI-MELODRAMAS

Another episode that takes only general inspiration from a movie original is "Disaster." It was obviously inspired by the spate of disaster films which appeared in the '70s, THE POSEIDON ADVENTURE, THE TOWERING INFERNO, AIRPORT films, EARTHQUAKE and others of that ilk. Picard is trapped in a turbolift elevator with a trio of tykes. He is finally able to convince them to work together, rather than whine together. Meanwhile, Troi finds herself inadvertently in command during this mini-disaster, and her commanding skills are put to the test.

Worf - trapped in Ten-Forward - finds himself shanghaied into the position of obstetrician, when O'Brien's wife Keiko starts delivering her baby (there is apparently a Writer's Guild regulation which says that all disaster stories must include a pregnant woman giving birth).

Elsewhere, Geordi and Dr. Crusher are trapped in a cargo bay and threatened by a radioactive fire. Riker and Data have to make it to Engineering to restore power. En route, Data must temporarily sacrifice his body.

Rather than one big story, "Disaster" is simply a series of mini-dramas or - perhaps, more accurately - mini-melodramas with simple solutions. There's a reason why the disaster film cycle died out, as "Disaster" amply demonstrates. The best aspects of the episode are the few character moments it provides, though Ensign Ro's (Michelle Forbes) hard-edged character is notably weakened in this one. Perhaps it will best be remembered as the episode where Troi got the chair and Picard got the shaft.

MIND CONTROL

"Disaster" was followed by a remake of a different type in "The Game,"

Patrick Stewart and Colm Meany at the Director's Guild premier of _The Snapper_.

a variation on Don Siegal's sf-horror classic INVASION OF THE BODY SNATCHERS (based on a novel by Jack Finney). In this instance, the bodies aren't being replaced by Pod People which is what Kevin McCarthy discovered in the original. Rather, the occupants of the Enterprise are having their minds enthralled to a highly addictive videogame (a situation, I'm sure, with which many parents can identify).

The infection spreads, after Riker is introduced to the game by a woman named Etana (Katherine Moffat) on Risa. He passes the game to Troi. Soon, it is replicated and spread throughout the Enterprise. Wil Wheaton returns to the show as Wes Crusher only to be assigned a Crusher cliché script; once more Wesley saves the Enterprise. The episode does have its creepy aspects, as everyone becomes a pusher for the game and tries to turn Wesley onto its pleasures. But he wisely decides to do some research on it first with his female friend Robin Lefler (Ashley Judd). Apparently, the two adolescents are the only ones who think of doing so. (Perhaps, it was all those anti-drug lectures they've been exposed to.) The story becomes too foolish to consider it seriously, and yet it gets too creepy to consider it a comedy.

Mind control also popped up in the episode "The Mind's Eye" which took the classic film THE MANCHURIAN CANDIDATE as its point of inspiration. In that classic movie Laurence Harvey was programmed by the Red Chinese to assassinate a political candidate to ensure James Gregory, playing a stooge for the Communist party and spouting McCarthyesque ravings, the Presidency of the United States. Frank Sinatra realizes that something is wrong. Everyone in Harvey's rescued platoon describes Harvey in exactly the same manner which is a description completely at odds with the man's actual personality. Sinatra figures out that when shown a special trigger (the Queen of Hearts), Harvey will follow any instruction given him. And so Sinatra realizes Harvey has been thoroughly brainwashed.

OUTER SPACE WESTERNS

In "The Mind's Eye" the Romulans have similarly brainwashed, none other than, Geordi LaForge who has been programmed to assassinate Klingon Governor Vagh. (La Forge receives his instructions through his VISOR on which he is so dependent. It is only Data's tracking of strange E-band emissions that clues him into what is going on). The STAR TREK episode lacks the satire or resonance of THE MANCHURIAN CANDIDATE, one of the most original and riveting films of the '60s. Particularly dramatic is the original's point-of-view shifts from the brainwashed soldiers viewpoint to the viewpoint of their Manchurian captors. "The Mind's Eye" is nowhere near as audacious, and La Forge's recovery from the experience is merely skimmed over.

Spaghetti western lovers were able to get a chuckle out of "A Fistful of Datas" with its title reference to Sergio Leone's A FISTFUL OF DOLLARS. The original film launched the trend in spaghetti westerns (i.e. Italian made westerns) as well as Clint Eastwood's extended career. (The original title of the NEXT GENERATION episode was to be "The Good, the Bad and the Klingon," itself a reference to Leone's THE GOOD, THE BAD AND THE UGLY). Once more the holodeck does something unpredictable and creates gunmen duplicates of Data who threaten Worf, Alexander and Troi. Once more Brent Spiner steals the show with his multiple incarnations of western stereotypes. Mercifully, Marina Sirtis' Troi is given a bit more to do than usual and certainly looks fetching in western attire. However, the conceit itself is very pinched and not sufficient to sustain much interest throughout.

What is it about science fiction TV shows? Eventually, they all attempt a pseudo-western. Classic Trek's "Spectre of the Gun"— which started from a very funny comedy script—was ridiculous when the situation was played straight. "Living In Har-mony," an episode of the classic series THE PRISONER, was a western (and so was the third installment of the BACK TO THE FUTURE film trilogy).

A MAN ALONE

Another generic recreation was "Starship Mine" in which Picard impersonates the character of Mott the barber (remember him?) and does a Bruce Willis/DIE HARD shtick playing touch and go with a series of terrorists who take over the Enterprise while it is docked at Remmler Array undergoing routine maintenance designed to eliminate all baryon particles. Picard's desire to escape the boring Commander Hutchinson (played by Steven Spielberg's brother, David) propels him to return to the Enterprise to retrieve his saddle and try out Hutchinson's stable of horses.

Like Willis' John McClane, Picard just happens to find himself in the right place at the wrong time when he espies one of the saboteurs about to take a laser welder to open a junction box. Having shed his formal Starfleet togs, he is not recognized as the captain by his adversaries who make the mistake of underestimating the little

bald "barber." Taking one of the men's communicators, Picard is able to eavesdrop on their conversations and plans, echoing McClane's use of the walkie-talkie in DIE HARD. There is an elaborate and enjoyable game of cat and mouse as Picard manages to outmaneuver the team which plans to take Trilithium waste which is only useful in weapons manufacture (much like the waste from our own nuclear power plants, which is otherwise highly toxic and undesirable). The literary antecedent for DIE HARD, which is where the film's story originated, is Roderick Thorpe's novel NOTHING LASTS FOREVER.

The loss of culture and the resumption of pride is the theme of both MALCOLM X and "The Birthright Part II." MALCOM X tells the story of former second-story man and drug dealer Malcolm Little who became, through the teachings of separatist black leader Elijah Muhammed, one of

Jonathan Frakes at Forest Lawn for the memorial of Gene Roddenberry.
Photo c 1994 Albert L. Ortega

the spokesmen of the black Muslims and rechristened himself Malcolm X rejecting the anglo surname given his slave forebears. By keeping to a strict diet, eschewing drugs and other stimulants and dedicating himself to developing his mind, Malcolm X became a dynamic public speaker who dared oppose the white power structure inspiring emulation in other young blacks who saw him taking on the power structure and winning moral victories to build a proud following.

A CULTURE LOST AND FOUND

In the STAR TREK version, set at a remote Romulan prison camp, Worf discovers that the young Klingons living there are ignorant of the true purpose of such war tools as the Klingon Gin'tak spear - having beaten them into proverbial plowshares. The Klingons here live in harmony with their former Romulan captors and don't challenge the status quo, but to Worf it is still a prison however comfortable it may be to its inhabitants. He constantly challenges the presumptions of the authorities and begins to teach Klingon pride and culture.

In yet another moment copped from CASABLANCA, Worf leads the Klingons in a lusty rendition of a Klingon victory song, which drowns out the sad lullaby version the Romulan-backed segment of the society were singing, echoing the classic scene where Paul Henried sings "La Marseilles" to drown out a nearby table of Germans. Despite integrating nicely into the Federation, Worf shows himself to be a Klingon separatist when it comes to Romulans, rejecting Ba'el whom he is highly attracted to simply because she is half Romulan. Ultimately Ba'el realizes that she will face prejudice wherever Klingons congregate, but that doesn't prevent her from siding with those who would leave their prison and rediscover their heritage at the end of the episode.

One of Worf's most powerful moments on NEXT GENERATION came in "The Enemy" where he balked at donating blood to save the life of a Romulan, preferring to let the man die. "The Enemy" itself was mostly inspired by the East-West one-on-one conflict of HELL IN THE PACIFIC in which Lee Marvin battles Toshiro Mifune who plays a Japanese soldier on a Pacific island during World War II. This film classic inspired Barry Longyear to write ENEMY MINE, a science fiction version which was turned into a film directed by Wolfgang Petersen.

A QUESTION OF LIFE

Probably the finest film-inspired episode of THE NEXT GENERATION is "Tapestry" which started life as a variation on the Dickens classic "A Christmas Carol," done innumerable times in films and television, only to end up as a brilliant variation on IT'S A WONDERFUL LIFE.

In IT'S A WONDERFUL LIFE, George Bailey (Jimmy Stewart) is suicidally depressed, because he has never been able to fulfill his dreams of getting away from Bedford Falls and exploring the world. By reviewing his life, a pair of omnipotent angels demonstrate what a mensch George Bailey actually is. He constantly sacrifices his own desires to assist the personal welfare of others and dedicates his life to his father's old savings and loan. That is the only place in town where the working man can borrow enough money to buy a house and live decently (of course, unlike today where the average working stiff isn't paid enough money to even qualify for a loan in many areas).

By showing him what life would have been like in Bedford Falls if he hadn't lived it, Clarence (Henry Travers) - the befuddled angel - demonstrates just how many lives he did touch which causes him an ecstatic readjustment. In essence, the film says that one's attitude is what makes all the difference between having a good life and a bad life. But in the highly sentimental scenes of kind friends coming through for the struggling Bailey, this message is often overlooked.

PAST MASTER

The message becomes more obvious in "Tapestry" in which Q plays God to a dying Picard and allows him to relive a moment that the mature Picard regrets—a barroom brawl with three Nausicaans. The rivalry cost Picard his heart, leaving him with a vulnerable artificial one. Apparently, Picard was quite the ladies man as a Starfleet officer, but his more mature self is less eager to indulge in experimental sexual liaisons, resulting in Picard's alienating three women in one day.

Cheated in the game of Don-Jot, Picard's best friend Corey (Ned Vaughn) swears revenge by planning to rig a game so he wins. Picard knows this will precipitate the near-fatal fight and tries to dissuade him - to no avail. Corey is confused by this more timid Picard and becomes angry with him. Jean-Luc's female chum Marta is impressed by the streak of responsibility suddenly appearing in Picard and offers to go to bed with him (another regret of Picard's is that they never had). However, sex only manages to screw up their friendship and proves a profound mistake in their previously close relationship.

In protecting Corey from the Nausicaans, it appears to Corey and Marta that Jean-Luc has betrayed them and submitted to the overbearing alien bullies. Springing from this alternate past to its cause-and-effect future, Picard finds himself a lieutenant, junior grade, an assistant astrophysics officer with a real heart and not much chance at promotion, because he has consistently been unwilling to take the risks involved. Picard realizes that this risk-taking element is what made him the starship commander that he was. That being less arrogant and undisciplined, as he wished his youth could have been, cemented him into being a "play it safe" nonentity, "a dreary man in a tedious job." What was wrong wasn't his life but his attitude towards it. The negative experience of near-death in his youth forced him to face his own mortality and focused him into becoming the man he really

Gates McFadden being honored at the Century Plaza by the Starlight Foundation. Photo c 1994 Albert L. Ortega

wanted to be.

THE NEXT GENERATION takes risks with unconventional episodes such as this one, and in doing so, I believe that it most excellently becomes the series that it aspires to be. While THE NEXT GENERATION employs a great deal of talent, both before and behind the camera, and looks to many different sources for inspiration—the movies being merely one of them—it remains an uneven show. However, as any long time watcher will tell you, at its best it ranks with the finest that television has to offer, giving us interesting insights into the problems that plague man, appealing characters who know how to work with - rather than against - each other. And sometimes it delivers to its audience the kind of fresh perspectives that only science fiction can offer.

—Dennis Fischer

THE ALTERNATE UNIVERSES OF TNG'S "PARALLELS"

One of the most intriguing possibilities in science fiction storytelling is the concept of the alternate, or parallel, universe. THE NEXT GENERATION recently demonstrated a new twist on that old, but popular, idea.

Season seven surprised viewers with an episode which explored, for the first time since "Yesterday's Enterprise" in season three, the alternate universe possibilities inherent in STAR TREK and did it in a dynamic and explosive fashion. Instead of one alternate universe, in "Parallels" we were introduced to the possibilities inherent in thousands of possible alternate realities with Worf as both guide and unwilling participant.

This masterwork weaves together bits of TREK history and entwines the viewer in the surreal journey Worf must make to return to his own universe. Like THE TERMINATOR and BACK TO THE FUTURE films, this episode exposes alternate realities in which every single choice and possible decision circles back on itself. This episode is quite moving and very disturbing.

Worf finds - like Will Riker in "Future Imperfect" and Beverly Crusher in "Remember Me" - he, alone, is conscious of changes in the way things are remembered and perceived. At first the clues are minor, but they multiply as Worf slips farther and farther away from our reality.

Worf is puzzled when odd shifts occur in his experience of reality as opposed to his memory of them: a cake is the wrong color, and Picard unexpectedly appears where he should not have. He dismisses these peculiarities. When Beverly tells him he lost a tournament—coming in 9th place—he sprints to his quarters to find his trophy and log altered. The Beverly in that universe thinks he is only suffering memory loss from a concussion. But Worf maintains his memories from one universe to the next. So odd transpositions in the fabric of reality occur, and Worf remembers each version. Picard seems to vanish from one universe to the

next, and Data and Geordi switch places from their accustomed posts in Engineering. Worf speaks of the events, but the alternate crew doesn't know what to think of Worf's perceptions.

THE COUNSELOR AND THE KLINGON

Worf and Troi are involved in each universe, weaving an unlikely love story that is heartbreakingly effective. Worf is talking with Troi in his cabin when Geordi enters, and he makes his first massive shift. Data's painting shifts across the room as Worf enters another universe. Troi's uniform and hair change, and the painting changes to a realistic work. Geordi had come to tell Worf that the evidence remembered in the other universe was not substantiated in this one. His VISOR, by emitting a subspace pulse, was pushing Worf further away from his home universe.

The final push came in Worf's worst nightmare. To be dazed at tactical dur-

ing a battle situation. To look down and find your boards reconfigured. Then looking around to see the bridge radically changed, engaged in conflict with the Cardassians. This universe loses its Geordi LaForge, who dies from plasma burns—since our Worf failed to activate the shields. Worf has now reached the end of what could be called the "close" universe.

He finds he did not attend the Batlath tournament, and is surprised when Troi enters his quarters, complains about the lock, makes herself at home—makes a sexual advance, then awaits him in his bed! He walks over cautiously, as she undoes his hair, massages his (naturally) tense neck, then begins to give him a kiss. He questions the appropriateness of her behavior and is understandably stunned to find out that now Deanna is his wife. The Deanna in this universe is the first one to believe him and he is amazed to see the love in her eyes for him. She takes

Working on the Borg ship for the episode _Q Who_.

him to Engineering, where Data tells him how he and Troi mated after his recovery from the spinal injury in "Ethics."

THE NATURE OF REALITY

Worf now sees how that might have happened. This Troi is called to sickbay, while this Data and our Worf realize that Geordi is the focal point of Worf's distortions. Worf is, by now, not amazed to find Dr. Ogowa instead of Dr. Crusher in sickbay.

He is also amazed to find Geordi dead—and realizes his inaction in this universe directly led to this death. Dr. Ogowa suggests the VISOR might play a part. When that Data activates the VISOR, the next act of the tragedy unfolds as Worf steps upon what could be called "The Enterprise of Broken Dreams." Worf doesn't even know where to begin. Dr. Crusher is again Chief Medical Officer, but that is about all that is familiar. They were apparently con-

ducting the exact same VISOR experiment in this, the pivotal, universe. Worf is now wearing a red uniform and soon finds out that he is Commander Worf, First Officer of this universe's Enterprise. A similar shield attack has killed this universe's Geordi, although this time the attack was by the Bajorans, fresh from their defeat of the Cardassians, no less.

Data and Troi are still helping him conduct the experiment. It seems the alternate Worf in the alternate universe was also in the process of being deflected by Geordi's VISOR. Worf should consider himself lucky he did not get transported again. If he had, it is doubtful he could have ever made it back. This particular universe has had more than its share of pain. Worf and Data explain the way the quantum signature of Worf is different and Data figures out how the universe jumping is occurring.

A UNIVERSE OF POSSIBILITIES

They explain it to the captain, a battle-steeled and saddened man, William T. Riker. This Riker has held the reins on the Enterprise-D for four years, but would give back every second of command if only he could have back the friend he saw die at the hands of the Borg. This Will Riker may not have been steeled by Guinan's hardening advice in "his" ready room. He may not have thrown away Picard's

book. He was somehow able to defeat the Borg, but he wasn't able to free Locutus from his hellish existence—except through death. Worf is lucky that in this universe Wesley Crusher was apparently forced to accept a field commission and move up to Lt. on the Enterprise.

Lt. Wesley Crusher, working with Data, was able to find the way to scan the quantum fissure in space and was searching for Worf's home universe through a complex system of multi-pattern sorting of the multiple quantum realities created by the quantum probability theory that states each probability does occur in separate quantum realities. His complex method of multi-reality time-string sorting is prepared to find Worf's home—when a Bajoran attack opens the fissure releasing all the other Enterprises into this universe.

Worf is greatly saddened at this Deanna's demeanor. He is again overwhelmed, this time when he finds out that this

love is far deeper than the one in the previous universe. In the last universe, Worf and Deanna fell in love after Worf's son, Alexander, brought them together during Worf's recovery from his spinal transplant. In this universe, they have been long-time lovers and are the parents of two young children, a 3 year old boy and a 2 year old girl. Worf learns that Alexander does not exist in this universe. The two embrace as she realizes she may lose her husband—her Worf—during the attempt to restore Worf to his proper universe. Two children may have to grow up without Worf for a parent, because of the trespass of this other Worf, who drove her husband into another universe. When Worf prepared to leave, he gave her a kiss for his duplicate, and gave a silent prayer her Worf would return.

TOO MANY ENTERPRISES

Wesley opens the subspace door which soon

becomes a Pandora's Box. When the Bajoran ship attacks, the blast forces open the fissure and every single possible combination of Enterprise-D begins to arrive.

Every single mission could have turned out differently. Different crewmen may have died. The number of possibilities is infinite. A simple measuring stick might be to imagine the universe in the Classic Trek episode "Mirror, Mirror" and multiply by 2.85 x 107. One jolt of comic relief comes with Wes' announcement of 285,000 hails being received by the Enterprise.

This Data notes the sector will be entirely filled with copies of the Enterprise, some very similar, some very distant. Some have similar crews and histories, some radically different. This is not to mention all the millions of possible universes in which the Enterprise was destroyed. It is staggering to try to comprehend just what might be in those many ships out there.

Many contain Picard and crew, while others have Riker and crew, while others—who can only guess? A Captain Jellico that kept the reins after Picard was tortured to death by the Cardassians. A Counselor Troi who led a plot to assassinate Picard. An Enterprise commanded by Lore, loaded with Borg that recently killed Picard and crew. The Bones of the Enterprise crew who failed to escape the booby-trap in "Booby Trap." An Enterprise where Data was destroyed, or never built. Jack Crusher serving as Picard's Number One, or a ship where Dr. Polaski is still CMO. Klingons, Romulans, Vulcans, Cardassians, Bajorans—all could be in command of ships commandeered.

WHEN THE LIVING MEET THE LOST

The Ferengi hijackers of "Rascals" may look across at the Ferengi of "Peak Performance."

Spock, McCoy and Scott are alive in some, dead in others, and the saddest of tales of all center on the Borg. Think how many of the Rikers played it safe when Picard was taken. How many didn't send the shuttle team to rescue Picard from Locutus? How many had a Data to read the Borg unimind, and a Picard with the will to get out the simple code word "sleep"?

In the Captain Riker of the Primary Alternate Universe we see a brave man who lost his best friend and is pleased to have a chance to see Picard again. He managed to survive in another timeline (ours and others.) Worf is hesitant to tell him of what a superhuman effort the other Riker made. If he even remembers it.

When "our" own Picard answers the hail, we see what this Will Riker has been going through for four years. How he must have tortured himself over his decision. Best he think the Picard he gazed on never met the

**Close-up of Klingon
hull.**
Photo c 1994 "Deep Focus"

Borg, than to contemplate the fact that this other Riker had done what he had not been able to do.

Think of Locutus. The odds are quite high that many of those other Enterprises out there were not able to defeat the Borg. Many of those ships might even contain their universe's Locutus with a Borg named Guinan. One shivers at the thought. Many of these Enterprise crews are from what we would consider evil Empires and unholy alliances. Every single possible combination. If there is one bad Enterprise, it is split back toward the good, with the same umber of probabilities.

THE FEDERATION—LOST!

As I reached this point in the tape of the episode, I backed up to examine the possibilities, then was blown away by the most disturbing face to ever grace THE NEXT GENERATION universe. A ship is firing on Worf's shuttle, the Curie. The alternate Riker, bested by the Borg in battle, but victorious in the war, then turns to his viewscreen and glances into a mirror. A mirror from hell. The Enterprise from hell. The Federation has fallen and the Borg have won.

This saddest of all Will Rikers has gone stark raving mad. A stunned 285,000 Will Rikers are forced to look hard and stare into their own eyes. If a single decision had gone the other way. . . The worst of all possible worlds.

In only four years, the Borg have managed to completely overrun the Federation and destroy humanity. The bridge looks just like the bridge on our Enterprise-D at the time of the Borg war—and how it would look now had the Federation lost that war. It is torn and destroyed, pushed beyond all endurance. This tragic wild-eyed Riker had escaped from hell itself and would not be pushed back for all the good will of all the other Enterprises combined. We can only hope Wes' torpedo put this nightmarish crew out of its tragic misery. I hope they were spared the singular hell that a return would bring. Not only to go back, but to realize you had a chance to escape and failed to. Those brave men and women have seen the worst world.

The alternate Riker who lost his captain felt relief he had not had to live this one's life. Quickly, he felt the steady fall of self-recrimination start to fall away. He was floored by the rush of empathy for the man who shared his face and, if not for a split-second decision, his fate.

LOST AND FOUND

This Will looked back at Deanna, who felt like she was going to die. Every ship that had a Troi, and that is most, had a Troi who was empathically linked with the other Trois, Wills and Worfs. She had to separate herself from her twins, forget the fact her husband Worf may be about to die, and that she might very well have to raise their two children alone. Now she is confronted by a sight that tears emotion from places she never even knew existed. Troi must look at a vision of her Will, her Imzadi and her Worf, her husband, following every worst case scenario she had imagined with another. The sheer pain of their pain was enough to overcome her. The Will in her

universe picked her up and placed her in the command chair. We can only hope that the slingshot effect through time erases her memories of the sight.

Tasha Yar lives on many of the ships, like the one that fought in the Klingon War that existed in the alternate universe in "Yesterday's Enterprise," which is this show's precedent. While that Tasha entered our reality, that ship was destroyed, but others that did not make the decisions which that Picard did would have thus appeared in the rift. Imagine a billion Guinans all scanning each other's souls and minds and dreams. The knowledge of what happened made Worf's head hurt.

When he successfully returned to our universe and dined with Deanna, he realized they were lovers and mates in multiple universes. Worf began to explain what had happened to him as he went further and further away from our reality. She would sit there with her mouth open as she heard

of the mating, the many deaths and the children, events that she never knew she had shared with Worf. At that moment Deanna began to see something in Worf that she had never seen before. Before she fell asleep that night, she shed tears for the Geordis and the Jean-Lucs who fell in other realities. And for the Worfs and Rikers who died in pain.

CONTEMPLATING THE POSSIBILITIES

She hoped with all her heart that her duplicate would be reunited with her Worf. Then Deanna looked at the stars. She thought of her many husbands and Imzadis in various realities and felt all their pain. She could not dwell on it, but she had to address it. Cold shivers would start down her back. She really enjoyed her dinner with Worf, but knew she would be haunted for years by the few details that Worf revealed. Still, Deanna was a professional in just about every universe. She marked

Worf down for extensive counseling sessions to come to grips with what he had to deal with. From universes with no Alexander to universes with other children, as well as the victorious Borg.

This could take some time. Then Deanna smiled. She thought that she would be spending more time with Worf after all. She fell asleep with a smile, thinking of how lucky she had it and wondering just what might have been. . .

Worf was just glad to find out that he had won the tournament after all. Had he really placed ninth, he wouldn't have wanted to return to his own universe. As Worf fell asleep, he dreamed of the other Deannas and his Deanna and Alexander. He dreamed of the children he had been denied by his own decisions. He had a brief vision of K'Ehyler, then the eyes of his Deannas. He decided that for a change, he thought counseling might not be so bad after all.

This is, perhaps, the most thought-provoking episode of THE NEXT GENERATION to date. It not only serves as a break-through episode that opens the imagination, it actually boggles the mind. A textbook case of The Uncertainty Principle in action. If any episode of THE NEXT GENERA-TION deserves to be nov-elized it is this one where-in the multiple realities can be explored in even greater detail. It will remain the single most talked about episode of the seven year TV history of STAR TREK—THE NEXT GENERATION.

—*Alex Burleson*

Patrick Stewart.   Photo c 1994 Albert L. Ortega

THE DIFFERENT STYLES OF STAR TREK'S COMMANDERS

How different are Kirk and Picard? Their careers have had some interesting parallels. Do their personalities have as many similarities as differences?

An organization's tone is often established by those at the top. Even Nixon admitted that the moral failings of his Presidency might have emanated from his failure to be a moral leader and to indicate that certain unethical behavior was not to be tolerated. The tenor of a business or school is often set by the man in charge, and so it is with the fictional chain of command in the first two versions of STAR TREK. Both Captain James T. Kirk and Captain Jean-Luc Picard are able leaders and heroic men, but each have their own style which consequently sets the tone of each series—Classic Trek and NEXT GENERATION.

The late, famed science fiction author Isaac Asimov described William Shatner's portrayal of Jim Kirk as "boyishly eager, open and vigorous. . . [T]he classic hero—young, strong, passionate, risk-taking." When STAR TREK announced that it intended to go boldly,

Shatner's Kirk perfectly embodied that claim.

By contrast, Captain Picard is more mature, more cerebral, closer to Spock than Kirk in temperament . He is a complicated man, seemingly the master of his emotions and apparently more open to taking counsel from his peers, but there is no mistaking his commanding presence and intention behind his frequent instruction, "Make it so."

If Roddenberry really meant it, when he claimed he sold STAR TREK as WAGON TRAIN TO THE STARS, then Kirk is the kind of cowboy one would expect from such a show. With his love-them-and-leave-them approach to women, he obviously has a touch of the rogue, seen also in his verbal play with semi-kindred (though more unscrupulous) spirits, Harry Mudd and Cyrano Jones. He takes obvious pleasure in out-maneuvering and out-thinking his enemies, giving a boyish smile whenever he looks back to a success or anticipates coming out on top. He is more mercurial, more apt to change from anger to laughter and back again than the more stable Picard, as well as more willing to use his phaser, though throughout most of the series he did evince a respect for most other life and life forms.

LEADING OR DELEGATING

Where Picard might delegate a task, Kirk takes charge. He leads the landing parties, at times rushing in where angels would fear to tread, undertaking personal risks with almost adolescent assurance in his own indestructibility. He clearly has an eye for the women, giving female yeomen and female aliens appreciative looks, but he seems to resist long-term commitments, hopping from one relationship to the next from week to week.

Contrariwise, Picard is more a politician and diplomat rolled up into one. Picard is obviously older and more seasoned, and is cool-headed where Kirk is hotheaded and eager. Picard is more politically correct in his respect of other genders and life forms, though strangely he sometimes seems less curious about learning from aliens than Kirk.

Even their speaking patterns are distinctly different. Kirk employs stretched out words and phrases interspersed with abrupt, clipped commands, like a rubber band stretching and then snapping. ("I. . . want. . . answers Mister!")

Though born in France, Jean-Luc enunciates common speech with a distinctly British accent and carefully modulated clear tones, the endings of which only become brusque when he is agitated.

Both men are perceived as sexy. Picard's phallic dome and rigid bearing denotes a commanding intelligence and masculinity, and his warm speaking voice gives clear indication of affection and sensitivity. Kirk is younger, virile, more of a swashbuckler who, with phasers blasting, can rescue fair maidens and sweep them away with his passionate stance. Even here Kirk is more the "man of action" while Picard tends to be the "man of thought."

EMOTION AND JUDGMENT

They both have had to sacrifice the women they loved, though for different reasons. Kirk sacrifices Edith Keeler so that her pacifistic ideas don't develop into a movement at the wrong time and allow the Nazis to create the atomic bomb first and win World War II. In Picard's case he has to separate his emotions from his judgment when he assigns Nella Daren ("Lessons") to a dangerous rescue situation, because he knows that she is the best person for the job. Sometimes being a commander means having to make sacrifices so that others might live.

While both men have their superhuman qualities, they each have their failings as well. Both men run on ego, convinced of their moral correctness in almost every situation, and both can be pompous and didactic, even boring occasionally.

Patrick Stewart and Jonathan Frakes at the Las Vegas Paramoung Booth VSDA Con.

Ron Moore, the best of the writers for THE NEXT GENERATION, in an interview in CINEFANTASTIQUE conducted by Mark Altman, compared the two commanders: "[Picard] and Kirk went through life quite differently. Kirk at the Academy was a bookworm, straight-laced, straight arrow and very uptight. You would call him a stack of books with legs—and then he became this wild man. He went out in the fleet and got comfortable and started doing all this crazy stuff. Picard went the other way. He was a wild man in his youth and then sort of became a little more mature and collected as he became an adult."

How differently would James Kirk have handled the situations Jean-Luc Picard found himself in? Obviously, this can be the subject of some speculation. Let's take a look at some of Picard's memorable missions and examine how he handled the difficulties they presented him.

PERSONAL BATTLES

When infected by the mysterious virus in "The Naked Now," Picard reveals his feelings for Beverly Crusher, not the strong attachment to his ship that Kirk evinced (which made it all the more mysterious when the Enterprise blows up in STAR TREK III—THE SEARCH FOR SPOCK; Kirk doesn't reflect ruefully on having to blow up his old home). In "Naked Now" the ship is nearly caught in the wake of a collapsing star, but disaster is narrowly averted. Still, both commanders were able to get a cure distributed and save the day and the ship, though Picard - thanks to Will Riker's memory - did have the advantage of being able to draw on the Enterprise's previous experience.

"Code of Honor" offers a few parallels to the Classic Trek episode "Amok Time," both of which offer crew members forced into a "fight to the death" (that ends up being rigged) in an alien culture. Picard allows Tasha Yar to fight, while in "Amok Time" Kirk is selected and would probably have insisted on fighting personally anyway. Picard respects the Prime Directive more than Kirk, who probably would have tried to argue that this particular element of Ligon culture be changed so that it would not destroy so many skilled members of that society.

Perhaps the most difficult to believe of Picard's decisions was the one he made in "Lonely Among Us," a weak, supposedly humorous reworking of "Journey to Babel" in which a possessed Picard decides to abandon his command and his ship and beam himself out into space to become one with yet another space cloud. While the desire to explore the galaxy is the basis of both series and both commanders, it's hard to picture Kirk suddenly deciding to pitch his responsibilities, abandon everybody he knows and go on a metaphysical quest within an alien entity. The B plot of squabbling delegates isn't very good either, and Picard would show a far greater mastery of the art of diplomacy in subsequent episodes.

COMMAND DECISIONS

Not only was Picard too ready to abandon ship, in "The Last Outpost" he is shown as too ready to surrender his ship to the Ferengi vessel. In STAR TREK III: THE SEARCH FOR SPOCK, Kirk does surrender the Enterprise with its minimal crew in a successful attempt to lure his enemies on board and destroy them. In STAR TREK VI: THE UNDISCOVERED COUNTRY to protect his crew he surrenders himself, but as Spock has pointed out, "There are always alternatives." Picard's decision seem needlessly hasty, especially when we finally see that the Ferengi aren't nearly the threat that they had been built up to be. The true cause of the Enterprise's distress is from the remnants of the

T'Kon Empire on the planet below.

Kirk probably wouldn't have had the same problems with violating the Prime Directive as Picard does in "Justice" where saving Wesley Crusher would have violated the Edo's right to set up their own system of justice. Instead, Kirk would more likely have rescued Wesley right away, not worrying his mother needlessly, and then begun lecturing the Edo on misuses of power. Picard - distracted by his conflict of ethics and a would-be, God-like creature - takes his time to make his point. Laws can't be absolute if there is to be justice. As Shakespeare pointed out long ago, "The quality of mercy is not strained/ It falleth like the gentle rain from heaven," meaning that it is not too difficult to sprinkle judgments with mercy, when it is called for; in fact, it's a divine thing to do.

"The Battle" is a more personal story for Picard as a wily Ferengi barrages him with a mind-control

device in an effort at revenge, because Picard's success at a Federation-Ferengi encounter resulted in the death of DaiMon Bok's son. Kirk, too, suffered under the effects of a mind-control device in "Dagger of the Mind." But both commanders end up turning the tables on their would-be tormentors. Data is forced to come up with an effective counter to the "Picard Maneuver" (no, it has nothing to do with straightening one's clothes after standing up) that could have saved Bok's son, had his commander thought of it. When Picard takes command of the Stargazer, he believes that he is reliving the battle of Maxia, and commands it to attack the Enterprise.

CONFRONTATIONS AND SACRIFICE

The concept of one's past catching up with one is fascinating, though Kirk had a more interesting time of it - when his oppo-

Patrick Stewart on opening night of Andrew Lloyd Webber's *Sunset Boulevard* at the Century City Shubert Theatre.
Photo c 1994 Albert L. Ortega

nent was the superior Khan Noonian Singh in STAR TREK II: THE WRATH OF KHAN - than Picard has with the relatively unimpressive Bok. (Only Patrick Stewart's performance keeps this illogical episode hanging together.)

While Kirk is likely to relax by going out wenching, Picard is more likely to take to the holodeck and relax by reliving a Dixon Hill scenario, as he does in "The Big Goodbye" and "Manhunt," tackle difficult literature such as James Joyce's ULYSSES or do some archeology as in "Captain's Holiday." Both commanders have doctors who tell them that they are working too hard - Kirk in "Shore Leave" and Picard in "Captain's Holiday" - shows them to be highly dedicated - if sometimes shortsighted - individuals who push themselves to the fullest.

In "11001001" and "Where Silence Has Lease," Picard threatens to blow up the ship, in the latter case with hundreds of families aboard, if aliens threaten to take his control away from him, echoing Kirk's decision in "Let That Be Your Last Battlefield." Still, the new Enterprise is a bigger ship with a greater emphasis on families, so I am not completely comfortable with Picard deciding to kill innocent people, rather than risk having them submit to possible alien torture, especially as he makes no attempt to get their view on the matter. Fortunately, the mysterious alien decides that, in seeing how humans prepare to meet death, it has learned enough about human beings and lets go.

And yet the supposedly ever-curious Picard makes almost no attempt to learn anything about this strange and powerful alien life form he has encountered, merely observing that both it and humans have a sense of curiosity, then leaving before exploring the source of that curiosity.

TORTUROUS ENCOUNTERS

Speaking of alien torture, Kirk is tortured by the Vians in "The Empath," one of the better third season episodes, in an effort to see if a Minaran, nicknamed Gem by Dr. McCoy, has the requisite empathy and compassion to risk her own life to save that of another, thus representing a race which is "morally" worthy of being saved. (Of course, the morality of torturing humans to achieve these ends does not seem to concern the mysterious Vians.)

Picard undergoes similar experiences in "Allegiance," "The Best of Both Worlds" and in "Chain of Command Part Two." In "Allegiance," he has been kidnapped by aliens and replaced by a not very effective double. Picard figures out that in order to closely observe his reactions, one of his fellow prisoners must also be one of his alien captors. In "Best of Both Worlds," Picard is given one of the most traumatic experiences of his life when he is converted into one of the Borg and leads the attack against the Federation, using his tactical talents to destroy much of Starfleet.

Perhaps most impressive is the powerful "Chain of Command Part Two" where Gul Madred (David Warner), a Cardassian torturer, unmercifully torments Picard in an effort to break him. (A fascinating study of the politics and psychological effects of torture is presented in THE BODY IN PAIN.) Like any man, even Picard can break under torture, although he doesn't lose his humanity or dignity.

The show received advice from Amnesty International, the world famous human rights group which reports on human rights abuses in countries throughout the world and which keeps up pressure on various governments to release (or at least not torture) political prisoners. Their help was incorporated in Frank Abatemarco's script, then it was rewritten by Jeri Taylor to concentrate on the character relationship between Picard and Madred. Picard is not tortured to supply information but simply forced to acknowledge the power of the torturer, which is more often the case in real life. It is a brutal power play, pure and simple, and given a tremendously powerful performance by Stewart.

INNER CHALLENGES

Kirk had a double in "The Enemy Within," a fascinating variation on the age-old Jekyll and Hyde theme where Matheson cannily asserted that men need both their dark and light halves to command and survive. Unfortunately, while the double which tries to seduce Beverly and sings drunken songs in Ten Forward allows Patrick Stewart to give an uncharacteristic performance in "Allegiance," the show is ultimately too derivative of basic conventions to be very interesting. And while the puzzle that causes a duplicate Picard to appear through a time paradox in "Time Squared" makes for an interesting mystery, it is never satisfactorily resolved.

One of Kirk's greatest moments of self-doubt was when he failed to fire at a deadly cloud creature that killed Captain Garrovick, his commander, and half the crew of the Farragut. The feeling of guilt that Kirk experiences pursues him, and he is only able to overcome it years later when he kills the creature with an anti-matter bomb after Spock has demonstrated to him that his failing to fire years before made no difference in the outcome.

Picard's great moment of self-doubt arrived when he was kidnapped by the Borg and turned into Locutus, leader of the Borg invasion, who leads a tremendously successful attack against Starfleet. He has his humanity restored after being taken from the Borg, where he is used once again, this time as a tool against the Borg. In the episode "Family," Picard returns to his roots in an effort to reorient himself and shake off that nightmarish experience. His exposure to his nephew Rene Picard reminds him of why he entered Starfleet in the first place rather than staying home and simply tending his own garden. Nevertheless, Picard is morally challenged in "I, Borg" when Picard uncharacteristically desires to let a young Borg die due to the extreme danger he potentially represents, though he accedes in Dr. Crusher's desire to care for him.

OF GODS AND MIND MELDS

While Kirk sometimes acted as if he were God, Picard gets mistaken for a god in "Who Watches the Watchers?" This ends up making him very self-conscious and uncomfortable, especially with the implications it has concerning the Prime Directive. Kirk has had an intense loathing of Klingons ever since his son was killed in STAR TREK III: THE SEARCH FOR SPOCK, and which was further explored in STAR TREK VI: THE UNDISCOVERED COUNTRY. But even if circumstances were different, it is unlikely he would have accepted being a Klingon advocate as Picard does in "Sins of the Father."

Both Kirk and Picard have experienced powerful Vulcan mind melds. When Spock tried to restore his memory in "The Paradise Syndrome," Kirk almost took over the mind fusion. One of the most powerful moments on THE NEXT GENERATION was when Sarek and Picard traded their consciousnesses, so that Picard could transact negotiations in the guise of Sarek while the tormented Vulcan lets loose his repressed feelings in a torrent of expression while in control of Picard's body (another acting tour de force by Patrick Stewart). In addition to Sarek, both Kirk and Picard have had dealings with Sarek's son, Spock—obviously for the former, his closest companion for whom he has risked his life and career. For Picard it was a brief meeting with a Starfleet legend engaged on the most important task of Spock's career in "Unification."

Both men have a knack for knowing their way around a courtroom and could have had alternate careers as lawyers, it seems, though again Kirk tends towards the dynamic while Picard remains maturely thoughtful. Picard is most effective when he counters Admiral Norah Satie's attempt at character assassination, thereby exposing her McCarthyesque techniques for all to see.

AN EYE FOR THE LADIES

Both Picard and Kirk do have a tendency to run into old flames—for Kirk there was Lt. Areel Shaw in "Court Martial," Janice Lester in "Turnabout Intruder" and Ruth in "Shore Leave," not to mention the numerous other women he flirts, beds, and/or falls in love with. For Picard, there is Jenice Manheim in "We'll Always Have Paris" and Captain Phillipa Louvois in "The Measure of a Man." While Picard is a more solitary individual, his good qualities do attract feminine attention, and not just from Lwaxana Troi, who delights in foisting her clearly unwanted attention on Picard (and being an empath, she can clearly read Picard's emotional response).

There is Vash in "Captain's Holiday" and

"Q-Pid"; Ardra in "Devil's Due," as well as Kamala (Famke Janssen), a genetic mesomorph whose duty is to be what any man wants her to be and who is engaged to the unpleasant Alrik even though she has fallen in love with Picard, because, unlike others, Jean-Luc insists that she has value in and of herself. There is also Eline in "The Inner Light" in which Picard gets to lead an alternate life (much as Kirk does in "The Paradise Syndrome") and gets to know the joys of being a husband and father. And finally there is Nella Daren in "Lessons," where Picard must deal with the awkwardness of falling in love with an underling and with the possibility of losing the woman he loves in the line of duty. As a consequence, Daren is forced to leave him despite her feelings.

Kirk and Picard both inspire feelings of admiration, loyalty, and love. When challenged with a moral dilemma, they effectively think their way to a reasonable solution.

When they choose to, they both can drip charm and charisma, but are also capable of being abrasive when that will bring out the best in a friend or the worst in an enemy. Both men represent heroes, role models, the kind of apotheosis of mankind that we all wish we could be. As a consequence, their popularity isn't difficult to understand. Each man has his own personal style, both men have dealt with similar problems. They are the kind of forceful commanders whose experience is considerable, whose compassion is boundless, and who cause millions of viewers the world over to tune in week after week. Wherever they lead, audiences are sure to follow.

—*Dennis Fischer*

CAPTAIN PICARD IN THE HOUSE: PATRICK STEWART MAKES THE TALK SHOW ROUNDS

Although the daytime talk shows have degenerated into a circus of dysfunctional personalities, the night time talk shows have remained what they started out to be—celebrity talk fests where people can see their favorite stars out of character. Patrick Stewart has shown himself to be a very entertaining guest. . .when he actually shows up (See the GOOD MORNING AMERICA chapter for the time he walked off in a huff).

Although most leading members of the cast of STAR TREK—THE NEXT GENERATION have appeared on talk shows throughout the show's seven-year run, few have adapted to the medium more readily than Patrick Stewart. Case in point: his frequent guest appearances on the ARSENIO HALL program. Over the last few years, Stewart and Hall have developed an easy rapport, and don't hesitate to play off the differences between the countryfied English gentleman actor and the streetwise American comedian.

On March 18th, 1992, Arsenio greeted Stewart with the news that someone Stewart knew had been on the show. "Captain! A friend of yours was here recently! Ben!"

"Mr. Kingsley?" inquired Stewart.

"You all are pretty tight, right?" asked Arsenio.

"We are," replied Stewart. "We have been for twenty-five years. We were bit part players in the Royal Shakespeare Company when we first came here in 1968, and I see him whenever he's in town."

Quick to joke about Stewart's baldness, Arsenio observed, "You all have similar heads."

"Here we go again!" Stewart cried, ready for the worst.

"Do people get you mixed up, ever?"

Stewart fielded this question gracefully, and recounted an amusing anecdote on the subject of baldness. "He was here two or three weeks ago, and I went to pick him up at his hotel. I have a convertible, and the top was down. He was waiting for me on the sidewalk, he got

in the car, and we drove down Beverly Boulevard and he said to me: 'You know, Patrick, anybody driving behind us would think Los Angeles has been invaded by an alien race!'"

To underscore this comedic point, Arsenio put pictures of Stewart and Kingsley up on the screen, and yes, there was quite a resemblance, and not just due to their baldness. "Now those two guys are supposed to hang out!" Here, as throughout the episode, the audience broke into laughter. Moving along and changing gears, Arsenio inquired about Stewart's daughter.

"How is she? Are you treating her right?"

"Well, I don't have a lot of opportunity. She's at school in England. But you are looking at a proud father tonight, not in connection with my daughter. Today is a very, very special day for me: my son, who graduated as an actor a few months ago, got his first television contract this afternoon." The audience applauded as Hall asked how Stewart's chil-

dren were doing.

"I always ask him about his daughter," he explained to the audience, "because he told me once about his daughter using slang, and he has a problem with that. And I say, as long as she understands the difference, there's nothing wrong with a little slang every now and then, y'unnerstand?"

INTERCONTINENTAL STORYTELLING

Stewart had a few thoughts on the subject as well. "The repercussions from that, Arsenio, went on and on and on, because her friends saw your show here and they phoned her in London and then her friends told her they'd seen it, and it was like, uh. . . We call it grandmother's whispers, where with each conversation the story gets changed a little bit. She thought that I'd been critical of her. Actually, I referred her to you. If you think I was critical, talk to Arsenio!"

Injecting a bit of absurdity into the proceedings,

Arsenio mugged a bit and cracked a few jokes. "I think when you're happy inside, it shows. I'm still ugly, but I'm happyyyy!!!"

"Well, where's the ugly part?" mused Stewart.

"I guess it's based on standards," explained Hall, "but I don't know. I shouldn't say that. Of course, at my house I live alone, and I look fine. Do people ever treat you differently because you're this proper Englishman with a Shakespearean background?"

Stewart indicated that they did. "I was talking with my colleagues on the show the other day about change, and how we change. By my age, I'm not supposed to change very much, and yet all my colleagues are convinced that has happened. Apart from the fact they claim that I've become Americanized; I feel that only means that I've become nicer. There was sense in which I think in the first year or two that I was here that people, when they met me, expected to find someone rather solemn, rather over-serious, and going on a talk show, people would think they had to treat me in a rather serious and somewhat dignified way. As you know, from personal experience, it ain't so."

A TOUCH OF INTROSPECTION

Arsenio took this opportunity to philosophize a bit. "Actually, you're yourself and I'm myself, and we kind of learn things from each other. I've learned about Anglophiles and you've learned a lot of interesting things coming to visit us. I want to ask you about an episode coming up on STAR TREK. They're gonna deal with sexual intolerance. I read that this morning."

"Not so much with sexual intolerance," clarified Stewart, "as the need for an individual's own sexual identity to be permitted to assert itself and to be independent. It's already become known as the 'gay episode,' but it's not specifically a gay episode. It does deal with a specific sexual inclination. But the show takes issues like this week by week."

"And that's an important thing to deal with. It gives new meaning to the word Klingon!" At this slightly off-color joke, both Patrick Stewart and the studio audience broke up with laughter. Arsenio continued: "But I think it's really important to deal with that. Let's talk about—" A second, louder wave of audience laughter interrupts him. "I'm sorry, that was a bad joke!"

"Now you've got it out," said Stewart, somewhat bemused. "That was the ugly part that was hanging around inside, now it's out!"

"Now I'm beautiful!"

THE CAPTAIN'S YACHT

Then Hall brought the subject to the Enterprise itself. "Let's talk about the spaceship. One quick question: if you could have some element of technology on that ship that it doesn't have, what would it be?"

"Not many people know about this; the captain's yacht. The ship has a yacht, and it's in all the design plans. It's a little kind of nipple at the bottom of the ship, and that's maybe inappropriate. . . I won't do that anymore—[referring to the gesture he made while describing the 'nipple'] and—"

"That's the ugly part in him!"

"And it's out! I don't need it anymore! Now I'm beautiful too!"

Stewart then composed himself after all this hilarity and started to describe another project he was involved in, a documentary about MGM studios. "It's a six-hour documentary about the history of Metro-Goldwyn-Mayer, and it's been more than two years in production. I play a kind of narrator, commentator, chorus figure, spirit of Metro-Goldwyn-Mayer. You should ask yourself, why is this Englishman playing

this role? It was the first question I asked. Metro-Goldwyn-Mayer was a very international lot at the time. [The show] consists of interviews with people, with stars, and employees of MGM, and clips, of course, because it's a Turner show, and Turner owns the MGM library. And then, the most stylish section of it is the commentary that, because we built a series of MGM-style sets which I inhabited in the company of a lion. For a couple of scenes we brought in Leo, the MGM lion."

THE TRUTH ABOUT LEO THE LION

"There really is a Leo?"

"No, his name is in fact Josie. He is one of the two authentic working lions in the United States, I'm told, and I spent days with him. It was a truly awesome experience. I have never heard a particular quality of silence and attention on the set as the first day that the trainer brought him on. If there was ever charisma in a perfor-

mance, this creature had it, even if he was just lying there. If somebody had to walk past him with a piece of furniture or a prop, whenever they went by him they would go. . ." At this Stewart indicates the movements of a person walking very, very carefully.

"He's stupendous. He and I had to make an entrance together. The idea was he would come down a ramp—we had to wait in the wings, he and I, just the two of us, side by side; this was a 350-pound lion. The idea was that he would go up a series of steps to a rostrum, stand there and go ROARRR, and I had to go around the front of him. Whenever we got to the bottom of the steps, he would just lean against me, and so the two of us would waive off to one side. We had become two good friends, I was told, and he didn't want to leave me."

On that note, this segment of the Arsenio show ended, moving on to a commercial and another guest.

Jonathan Frakes with Genie Francis.
Photo c 1994 Albert L. Ortega

TOGETHER AGAIN

Four months later, on July 23rd, 1992, Stewart appeared on ARSENIO again. As ever, he was relaxed on this talk show which is shot on the same Paramount lot as STAR TREK—THE NEXT GENERATION—so relaxed that he forgot what he'd talked about on his previous appearance. Arsenio introduced Stewart with a reference to a most singular honor the actor had recently received.

A Next Generation Celebration   **83**

Levar Burton at the Armand Hammer Museum in Westwood with wife Stephanie Cozart at an unveiling for artist Yamagata, hosted by Arnold Schwarzenegger.
Photo c 1994 Albert L. Ortega

"Along with Cindy Crawford, my next guest shares the cover of the week's TV GUIDE as the readers' choice for most bodacious duo. . . got it?"

"I know what you're gonna ask!" exclaimed Stewart, pretending to be defensive.

"They use the word 'bodacious'—first of all, is that a real word?" asked Arsenio. "And have you ever used it in your life before this?"

"I've never used it, I never heard it before and I didn't know what it meant. I can't find it in the dictionary."

"Somebody told me they did find it today."

"Webster's. I have the

wrong dictionary. I have one of the English dictionaries."

"Those are out now!"

"Well, that's what you were going to ask. . . how does it feel? Well, it feels better than being the man with the worst halitosis in the world. It feels better than being the man with the flattest feet in the world. And very surprising. But I wish I had been voted it when I was sixteen or seventeen. I was a very unconfident teenager. And whatever they voted for— and thank you, all of those who voted for me—in part, they voted for confidence. Don't you think? Self confidence, mostly, is attractive."

"Are you very self-confident?"

"I have a little more than I used to have; you do, too. In the year that we've been meeting here, it's changed."

THE OPPOSITE SEX

"When you were young, do you remember your first girlfriend?"

"I remember my first crush. But it never developed into a girlfriend. I could never make that step into asking somebody out. I was talking to a friend the other day about sitting in the back row of the movies waiting for the right moment, not quite knowing when it would be, and sometimes getting through the whole movie and never, ever taking that risk. I was very, very shy, and very insecure around girls."

"Who are your friends? Who do you hang out with?"

"This was a girlfriend I was talking to," Stewart confessed, "this was my girlfriend I was talking to. . . well, my friends? The crew of the show. They're my best buddies, and I have friends here in Los Angeles from before STAR TREK. I used to do a lot of teaching and lecturing, and I have friends at UCLA: teachers, professors. By the way, I'm not going to make any reference to the coats. I just want you to know, I have

too much good taste to make reference to your coat! I wouldn't say a word about his coat, at all." As usual, Arsenio was dressed in a fairly flashy manner, especially when compared to the relatively sedate-looking Stewart. Now comes the moment when Stewart slipped up. . .

IF IT WAS FUNNY THE FIRST TIME. . .

"Don't you party with Ben Kingsley or something?" Hall asked.

"Yes, we've been partying and acting together for twenty-five years or more. We were. . . I didn't tell you this story, did I? I'm sure I didn't. . ."

Actually, he did tell this story—on his previous appearance on Arsenio's show. But this doesn't deter him from repeating it almost verbatim, right up to the punchline: "You know, Patrick, if anybody's driving behind us, they'll think an alien race has invaded town." Fortunately, the studio audience was not the same one from the previous show, and they laughed appreciatively. Arsenio laughed along too, although it wasn't entirely certain that he remembered that this was a repeated story or not. This, of course, is one of the hazards of being a talk show guest: this was clearly a favorite story of Patrick Stewart's, the sort of memorized anecdote he's probably trotted out several dozen times or more in his public appearances. "Yeah, we look almost like brothers," Stewart continued, referring to the baldness shared by both British actors. "I mean, brothers—"

"I know what you mean! You've got very hip since you've been visiting!"

"Oh yes! Thanks to you!"

"What kind of fan mail do you get? I got a feeling that your head is what women find sexy." The female members of the audience let out a collective whoop at this.

"Well, yeah, that's gratifying to me because I lost my hair when I was nine-

teen. It was a traumatic experience, and I thought that no woman would ever look art me again because of that. What I discovered is, if you have little, make it as little as possible."

THE DIFFERENCE WITH AMERICANS

"What kind of fan mail. . ." Arsenio asked again.

"On the whole, very pleasant fan mail. And it does surprise me, though, how some fans can write very personal, very intimate stuff in a letter to a complete stranger."

"It's the American way."

"You're right—the American way is to be much more open, much more frank, much more free with your emotions, to confess how you feel to people more frankly than the British do. I think that has been the major change in my life since I came to live here. I feel much more relaxed now."

Arsenio then prepares to show a clip from "Inner Light," the NEXT GENERATION episode in which

Captain Picard lives another man's life, and has a daughter and a son. The scene involves Picard's son, played by Stewart's actual son, telling his father that he's decided to pursue his music.

"You're working with your son now and then?" asks Arsenio by way of introduction. "That's cool."

"It is cool," replied Stewart. Suddenly he caught himself, bemused once more: "Did I say 'cool'?"

STAR TREK IS COOL

"Yeah, you did," said Arsenio, as the audience laughed. "That's funny to us," he explained, "because when he first came here he used to talk about how his daughter watches the show, and—" imitating Stewart, but not terribly well—"'I try to get her not to use words like 'dissed'— what does 'dissed' mean? How do you 'dis' someone? I tell my daughter, don't use these words!'" This has the audience fairly in stitches, so Arsenio continues, portraying Stewart as affecting a hip slang persona: "Yeah, STAR TREK is coool!"

"If I were wearing your coat, you would see a complete transformation."

"If I could get this mike off, you would be wearing my coat. 'Cause I would love to see you like this, and when the riots start, you'd be safe! 'Patrick Stewart—naw, that's that bald brother lootin'!'" [This was shortly after the LA riots in the wake of the first Rodney King police brutality verdict.]

"I've thought about that, and I just wonder how the rioters might have reacted to Jean-Luc Picard. That wouldn't have crossed your mind—why should it?"

Arsenio smoothly segued into asking Stewart where he'd been during the riots. Stewart, it seems, had been driving into Los Angeles from the north, unaware that the riots in the wake of the first Rodney King verdict were ravaging parts of Los Angeles. Someone called Stewart on his car phone and informed him of the situation, to which Arsenio quipped: "And you were on your way in to get some barbecue in Compton or somethin'!"

Stewart was quick to riposte: "And you thought I didn't know where Compton was!"

PATRICK AND SON

Arsenio finally got around to showing the clip of Patrick Stewart and his son in "Inner Light." It's a good scene, and the audience applauds appreciatively—only to double their applause when Stewart's son comes out on stage.

"This is bodacious, man," he says as he steps out to join his father and Arsenio. "Bodacious. . . y'know, I wanna know who was on that panel of judges ."

"What panel of judges?" intoned the elder Stewart. "It was—THE PEOPLE!"

Arsenio then remarked that Mark Stewart looked different with his glasses on, and almost comments about the younger Stewart's own fading hairline, as well. It seems that Mark had extra hair applied for his role on THE NEXT GENERATION.

"It was a great thrill to do that show," exclaimed Mark. Ever the cynic, Arsenio inquired if Mark had to read for the role. "Yeah, I did," he replied, in mock outrage. "What, are you suggesting nepotism in this town? I resent that, Mr. Hall!" The segment then ended with a few more references to Patrick Stewart as "Mr. Bodacious," and this episode of Arsenio, which featured a particularly relaxed and engaging (despite the repeated anecdote) Patrick Stewart, went on to its next guest.

MORE TALK, ANOTHER HOST

Patrick Stewart also appeared on the short-

Gates McFadden at the 1992 Creation Con Q&A with cast.
Photo c 1994 Albert L. Ortega

lived, if somewhat sloppily entertaining, Dennis Miller Show. Miller had an engaging personality as a comedian and commentator but interviewing was never really his strong point. He never seemed entirely at ease with most of his guests, although he did try in earnest. While one can easily point out that Arsenio Hall is not, in any journalistic sense, a very insightful interviewer either, he does excel at putting his guests at ease, as demonstrated by Stewart's greater relaxation every time he's been on the show. Stewart's DENNIS MILLER appearance makes for an interesting contrast.

When Stewart made his way to the stage and made an offhand comment about finding his way to the show, to which Miller quipped "You're used to being beamed places."

ENTERTAINMENT WEEKLY had just done a STAR TREK piece which billed Stewart as one of TV's most improbable sex symbols, which Miller brought up immediately. Stewart brushed that off affably and explained his earlier comment—when he had gotten into his car to drive to the show, his car didn't start, and, as he put it, he suddenly became "a savage. I drove from the Valley, to here, in my son's truck. He drove it out to me because I'm too mean to get a taxi. (Note: here Stewart is using the word "mean" in a British sense of the word, meaning "cheap" rather than having a hostile personality.) "You people offered me a car, but I rejected it."

Mining the Trek angle for all he could, Miller asked Stewart what had happened to his own car:

"Faulty dilithium crystals?" At least Miller had the decency to comment on his own material: "He's been out here twenty seconds and I've done every lame STAR TREK joke I know! I'm sorry!"

Stewart was quite relaxed, however, and had no problem with all this. He went on to reveal his own failing of the day: he had driven all the way to Hollywood with the hand brake of his son's car still on.

TREK AND POLITICS

Miller moved on to an easy question: he asked Stewart if he'd been prepared for the impact of the show, and Stewart once again trotted out his usual story about the different attitudes to STAR TREK in the US and Britain. Miller then asked: "How many whacked people do you meet a day over here who want you to put them in the ship to take them away and save them from their lives?"

"There are Trekkies that are mad for it," explained Stewart, "and there a lot of people who would not classify themselves as Trekkies who are mad for it, too. It is one of the delightful curiosities of the show that it does span all ages, all races, all educational backgrounds or social backgrounds, and it's a compliment to the show."

After a commercial break, Miller, to his credit, turned the focus to non-Trek matters, and asked if Picard's knowledge of political matters paralleled that of Patrick Stewart. Stewart agreed that it was, indeed, so. "I was brought up in a family that was politically active," he revealed, and actually sang a fragment of a political candidate's campaign song that he first performed on the street corner at the age of eight or nine. Miller then inquired about Stewart's opinions on the American political system. Stewart was quite outspoken, and was obviously pleased to have been asked.

"For the second time," Stewart began, referring to the then-current presidential race, "which is an indication of how long our show has been running! We're going through the election of, well, I assume it will be a second president." This assessment drew cheers from the crowd (obviously not comprised of the same folks who attend tapings of the Rush Limbaugh show). "There are still things about it that I don't understand," confessed Stewart; it seems he doesn't really get the concept of the presidential primaries.

ON STAGE

After Miller made a political joke, Stewart himself changed the subject by bringing out a newspaper clipping a fan had sent him that week. It was a copy of Patrick Stewart's first stage review, at the age of twelve—complete with photograph. (And yes, he did have hair when he was twelve.) Miller read the passage aloud at Stewart's request: "Patrick Stewart had nice movement, but not enough variety. . ." That was basically it, too, a very brief mention. The talk then moved to Stewart's latest stage work, his one-man rendition of Charles Dickens' "A Christmas Carol." When Miller asked if Stewart had been nervous in approaching his first Broadway production, Stewart replied: "It almost seemed the very first thing I was going to do on a Broadway stage was vomit! It was a solo show; there was just me and thirty or forty different characters just waiting for me on stage; characters that I had to inhabit."

"Which one was going to vomit?" asked Miller, segueing neatly into a reference to George Bush's then-recent faux pas in Japan.

"I'm not sure that that's the kind of company I would like to keep," observed Stewart, obviously not a big fan of the incumbent president. More applause followed this statement. After plugging, again, his MGM special, Patrick Stewart wound down his single appearance on THE DENNIS MILLER SHOW. Despite Miller's awkward style, Stewart was quite self-possessed throughout, having obviously mastered the art of being the talk show guest by this point in his career. As the show faded to a commercial, a member of the crew handed Stewart a drawing he'd done of him, and Stewart accepted it graciously.

And this time he didn't tell the Ben Kingsley story.

ANALYSIS OF THE PRIME DIRECTIVE IMPACT ON STARFLEET STABILITY

It is a dilemma that awaits every Starfleet officer - at some time in their career - they will face down the Prime Directive: General Order Number One. It is an eloquent method of learning from history's mistakes and attempting to stay out of the lives of indigenous beings that are not yet ready for contact with the many space-going races of the Federation. It is a proud and a sensible plan, but it is also a plan involving both death and destruction.

The words are simple and pure, fresh in the legal language of the 23rd century, years after the legalese had been stripped from the law-books, simplifying matters and allowing any person to serve as his or her own attorney.

Many a captain failed to grasp the meaning of these simple words until it was too late. Good intentions were no more effective an excuse than negligence or ignorance would be.

The Prime Directive was in direct conflict with the concept of unrestricted contact with any other culture. In the purest sense, when dealing with the most primitive of cultures, it is a directive which is easy to live with. When a captain must stand by and watch millions die, as entire races scream their death-cry, he or she must turn a deaf ear.

Starfleet Command has been ordered to obey the Prime Directive by the Secretary of Starfleet. It was recommended by an earlier Secretary and passed as a series of executive orders by the full Federation Council. The 6 General Orders are quite specific in regard to the extent with which they pertain to all Starfleet personnel. This allows the Federation Council and Assembly to maintain control over the military, while conversely, they also allow Starfleet the capability, through its actions, of influencing interplanetary relations with other species. The commander of a vessel makes the decision on the spot, yet he or she will answer to Starfleet and the Federation Council if the conduct is questionable.

The Prime Directive is as follows:

GENERAL ORDER NUMBER ONE

As the right of each sentient species to live in accordance with its normal cultural evolution is considered sacred, no Starfleet personnel may interfere with the normal and healthy development of alien life and culture. Such interference includes introducing superior knowledge, strength or technology to a world whose society is incapable of handling such advantages wisely. Starfleet personnel may not violate this Prime Directive, even to save their lives and/or their ships, unless they are acting to right an earlier violation or an accidental contamination of said culture. This directive takes precedence over any and all other considerations, and carries with it the highest moral obligation.

GENERAL ORDER NUMBER FOUR

If contact is made with hitherto undiscovered intelligent life-forms, under no circumstance shall Starfleet personnel, either by word or deed, inform said life-forms that worlds other than their own, or intelligent life-forms other than their own, exist outside the confines of their own space.

GENERAL ORDER NUMBER TEN

If there exists eyewitness testimony by senior officers or similar verifiable evidence that an individual has violated the Prime Directive, said individual may be relieved of duty by a duly sworn representative of the Federation government and placed under immediate arrest. The government representative shall then take such action as he deems necessary to minimize the results of the violation.

GENERAL ORDER NUMBER FOURTEEN

Starfleet personnel may intervene in local planetary affairs to restore general order and to secure the lives and property of Federation citizens only upon receiving a direct order to do so from a civilian official with the title of governor or higher.

GENERAL ORDER SIXTEEN

Starfleet personnel may extend technological, medical or other scientific assistance to a member of a previously unrecognized sentient species only if such assistance in no way compromises the Prime Directive or the security of the Federation or Starfleet.

GENERAL ORDER TWENTY-THREE

When verifiable proof is presented to the senior commanding officer of a Starfleet vessel or post that a Federation representative may currently be acting or have acted in the past to violate the Prime Directive, the officer may relieve said representative

of office, then assume the full power of that office pending a full investigation by government officials.

THE DIRECTIVE INVOKED

The first man to face the Prime Directive was a brash young captain named James Gunther Smithson, a bearded wild-eyed tactical genius. Smithson was born in Bremanhaven in the United States of Europe. He holds the unenviable distinction of being the first Starfleet officer to be court-martialed for violating the Prime Directive. On Stardate 1.2803 (old system), Smithson's vessel entered the orbit of Vega Proxima. Two rival power blocs were about to unleash a nuclear war which would annihilate all life on the heavily populated, technologically advanced planet. Smithson used his ship's phasers to destroy the thermonuclear fusion weapons before they

reached their targets. The actions by Captain Smithson saved billions of lives. It also cost him his command.

Captain James Gunther Smithson was relieved of command of his starship and dishonorably discharged from Starfleet. He later died in an accident. The Federation Council took into account the favorable outcome of the intervention in deciding not to sentence Smithson to prison. He was the first, but certainly not the last, Starfleet captain to find the Prime Directive in his path. While it is a noble ideal, it is also one that is capable of ripping your heart out no matter what path you choose.

—*Alex Burleson*

Working on the Borg ship for *Q Who.*
Photo c 1994 "Deep Focus"

SCIENCE AND THE NEXT GENERATION

STAR TREK has served to both revitalize an interest in science in upcoming generations as well as explore ideas which may well come to pass because of young minds who were sparked by what STAR TREK suggested was possible.

The reason STAR TREK—THE NEXT GENERATION is such a treasure lies not only in its considerable entertainment value, but in the program's ability to spark the imaginations of the people all over the planet who watch it. Like the parent Enterprise, the new ship and crew have unlocked the minds of those who join them for each adventure. Many major scientific breakthroughs and advances could be based on ideas that scientists might have seen on STAR TREK, then adapted into a feasible working prototype.

SPACE MEDICINE

U.S. Navy vessels now have a sick bay which features a full bio-medical monitoring board, just like Bones used on the original Enterprise.

An article in the Houston Chronicle from Reuters News Service quoted a military strategist discussing the Pentagon's push to develop a non-lethal weapon. The reporter wrote that the proposed "kinder, gentler" weapon would feature a "Stun" and "Kill" setting—just like the phasers on STAR TREK.

Medical researchers are working on cancer cures that are very similar to those described in THE NEXT GENERATION. Dr. Crusher's work on microscopic disease fighting weapons called "nanites" may be centuries away, but doctors are today trying to eliminate disease with micron-sized weapons which could kill the individual mutated cell, changing the deadly growth into an inert gas while leaving the surrounding tissue unharmed. A far cry from "20th century medieval medicine," (as McCoy bluntly put it), where some patients are poisoned with chemicals and radiation in hopes that the treatment will kill the disease before it kills the patient.

With the newly proposed techniques being tested, the disease could be "surgically" removed, one deadly cell at a time. A cure to most cancers may be found in an idea sparked by what a scientist saw while watching THE NEXT GENERATION— an idea that crosses the line from science fiction into science fact.

The creators and producers of STAR TREK— THE NEXT GENERATION will never know how many real-life "Wesley Crushers" will one day make a breakthrough in the science of microbiology, thereby allowing doctors to get at the patient's medical problem directly. And STAR TREK's influence can be seen far beyond medicine.

TODAY'S FANS, TOMORROW'S SCIENTISTS

The various incarnations of TREK have inspired students in electronic and computer programming fields, with many of today's brightest students being introduced to concepts that can be applied in sciences as varied as quantum chromodynamics, quantum electrodynamics, quantum mechanics, general relativity, astronomy, astrophysics, biology, exobiology. . . the list is endless.

Many writers and people who work in television were first inspired to put pen to paper by STAR TREK. Many other casual fans developed a working knowledge of the TV industry through the study of TREK. Science is but the most notable field of study vision that the logical shows help to broaden.

The proposed form of 24th century physics postulated on THE NEXT GENERATION is as far removed from our Newtonian/Einsteinian physics as we are from Galileo's and Galileo was from Ptolomy. THE NEXT GENERATION and the science presented there builds on Classic Trek's expected discovery of the multi-dimensional succes-

Close-up of "scorch" areas.   Photo c 1994 "Deep Focus"

sor to our current transistor technology. It is all in perceptions.

The development of transtator technology, presumably some time in the 22nd century, opened up the world of subspace, allowing a way to travel in multi-dimensional directions, warping space to allow the appearance of travel faster than the speed of light. The multi-dimensional nature of dilithium then opened up a second periodic table of the ele-

ments and led to forms of science not yet founded. Computers improve as deutronics revolutionizes the emerging science of dynamics leading to true artificial intelligence.

TREK TECHNOLOGY

While some mistakenly believe that the warp nacelles are merely propulsion engines, in TREK terminology, they are actually time and space warping particle field con-

verters which allow the ENTERPRISE to enter "warp space", where the ship never matches the speed of light in "real space," so the ship never reaches infinite mass.

If you think seven-dimensional calculus is convoluted, just look at the current pace of technology. If you use a computer modem, you are using a piece of equipment that uses a method of eight-dimensional spacing to transfer information at

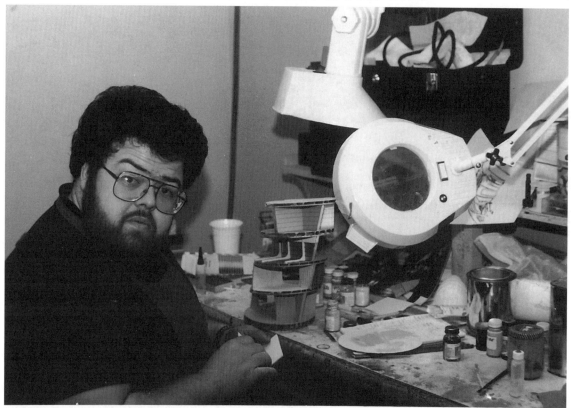

Kim Bailey working on "core sample" from *Q Who*. Photo c 1994 "Deep Focus"

a much higher speed. To accept TREK technology is not to leave science behind, but to embrace it and build on it.

In his outstanding quantum cosmology tome, DEEP TIME, author David Darling follows a single proton from the Big Bang to the Big Crunch. In his novel, he speculates about both transporter technology and faster-than-light starships. He suggests that five-mile long starships might be common. His analysis never mentions THE NEXT GENERATION, but his theoretical constructs could have just as easily come from methods employed on THE NEXT GENERATION by Data or Geordi.

Aristotle and Ptolomy started the search. Newton, Galileo, Kepler, Brahe and others laid the ground work. Then in the early 20th century, Albert Einstein led us into the subatomic world along with Max Planck and quantum mechanics. That revolutionary new set of both special and general theories of relativity, combined with the realization that matter and energy are just different forms of the same thing ($E=mc2$), when coupled with the discovery of quantum mechanics, opened the door to chaos theory, multiple supersymmetry and superstring constructions that challenge us to live up to the potential for discovery.

FASTER THAN LIGHT

Astrophysics legend Stephen Hawking realized

this. His work has led the way to remarkable discoveries. His realizations include the theory that black holes emit "Hawking Radiation" as virtual particles are torn asunder and the detected one fails to annihilate with its antiparticle which entered the singularity after crossing the event horizon of a Schwarzchild Black Hole. (In a Kerr rotating black hole, the event horizon would be a ring penetrable into a so-called "anti-universe." In his book A BRIEF HISTORY OF TIME (FROM THE BIG BANG TO BLACK HOLES), the quantum cosmologist speculated on various theories on multidimensional shifting. That might open the door to eventual Faster Than Light travel, proposing a ship, in effect, shrinking into a chaotic strange attractor, an infinite point, then emerging light-years away. In THE WOUNDED SKY, Diane Duane uses this theory to enter deSitter Space, the Classic Trek crew would travel through a

singularity into the space which contained no matter. Thus deSitter used the space as a mathematical curiosity to explain galactic growth rates, until Einstein realized its contribution (when combined with the Reimann geometry of curved surfaces and Markowski's four-dimensional view of a true space-time continuum with three spatial dimensions and one temporal dimension). To cancel out all the infinites, eleven dimensions are required and in some cases expand up to twenty-five dimensions. So as convoluted and fantastic as the science in THE NEXT GENERATION sometimes appears, 20th century theorists and mathematicians are already postulating concepts which are even more fantastic.

On THE NEXT GENERATION, Lt. Reginald Barclay debated Grand Unification Theories (attempting to reconcile gravity with the strong and electro-weak nuclear forces) and Einstein

appeared in a holodeck poker game with Sir Isaac Newton and the real Dr. Stephen Hawking. Hawking told the punchline of a joke that concerned the first classical test of Einstein's then controversial new theory. The proof was supplied when the perihelion of Mercury being off 43 arc seconds per century was explained by general relativistic effects caused by the gravity well of Sol on Mercury, which is much like a moon to the yellow dwarf, as Sol builds tidal pressure on Mercury which always keeps the same side to the sun, as the moon does to Earth.

POINTING TOWARDS THE FUTURE

The theory was further bolstered by measuring the gravitational effect of the sun in warping rays from distant stars. The Einstein redshift was proven with the discovery of the first binary pulsar in 1974, while the use of a laser beam to measure elapsed time in space allowed for the proven relativistic effects of gravity on space-time. The science of today is building the bridge to STAR TREK, just as the real technology of special video effects is being perfected by the master artists at THE NEXT GENERATION, who combine art with science to weave a mosaic, a tapestry of what we can only hope to live up to.

In THE NEXT GENERATION novel SPARTACUS by T.L. Mancour, the Enterprise encounters a cosmic storm, described as "the Gabriel Effect" (after Captain Gabriel).

"A reaction of certain electro-magnetic energies with a very specific kind of gravitational field such as that caused by a cosmic string, perhaps, or even a naturally occurring space warp. Reality mechanics had something to do with it, they hypothesized, but both fields of study were still so new and theoretical that there was no language, let alone rules or laws, to describe the theory."

And that was from a 24th century perspective.

Magic becomes physics only when it is understood. STAR TREK doesn't just break the laws of physics —it appeals them to a higher court. We can't explain what we don't know enough about to look for, we can only speculate and continue to learn a little bit more every day.

THE NATURE OF SCIENCE

In Margaret Wander Bonanno's STRANGERS FROM THE SKY, Panjeb, an Egyptian who travels through time in reverse, says, "One person's hocus-pocus is another's science, and a third's religion."

THE NEXT GENERATION has excelled at opening the minds of its viewers to the myriad possibilities which exist in this universe. And only in this century have we been able to begin to understand the tapestry which connects every object on this planet to the stars. What higher compliment can you give to a television show than to say that it teaches kids of all ages to open their

minds and learn to think. To learn just for the thrill of gathering new knowledge. This enthusiasm can only increase as students take time to look up a term they heard on THE NEXT GENERATION, or ask a teacher about some question they had about it.

The STAR TREK phenomenon, led by THE NEXT GENERATION in the 1980's and the 1990's, has exposed some students to wild thoughts that may have moved them toward a career in science and joining in Terra's never-ending quest for knowledge. In that respect, the search for the answer to the questions raised on TREK is endemic to the human condition.

RODDENBERRY'S LEGACY

The reach of THE NEXT GENERATION into the mindset of today's popular culture is best illustrated by a recent article in USA TODAY which credits STAR TREK with "turning kids on to science." The article is testimony to what STAR TREK creator Gene Roddenberry managed to accomplish and to the rare legacy he has left to the children of today and the children of the future.

Appearing in the January 4th, 1994 edition, it is headlined "SCI-FI TURNS KIDS ON TO SCIENCE," and goes on to state, "Kids say their love of science is sparked more by the STAR TREK TV series than by teachers smashing chemicals with mortar and pestle, a new survey shows. When 30,000 students in Indiana and the Chicago area were asked who or what most influenced their interest in science, the kids gave top rating to STAR TREK—THE NEXT GENERA-TION and the original STAR TREK. Parents finished second, teachers third."

"Whether it knows it or not, the entertainment industry is stimulating the imaginations of these students," says Harry Kloor of Purdue University's physics department, which conducted the survey.

The remaining top 10, in order, has scientists and stars.

- BEAKMAN'S WORLD, a comic, TV science show.
- NASA and the astronauts.
- Movies by Steven Spielberg and George Lucas.
- TV's MR. WIZARD
- Authors Michael Crichton, Isaac Asimov and Carl Sagan.
- British scientist Stephen Hawking.
- Marvel Comics characters like X-Men and Spider-Man.

THE FUTURE BEGINS TODAY

STAR TREK keeps alive the eternal struggle—the eternal dream we have of reaching the stars. These fusion reactors not only forged the iron in our blood and the calcium in our bones—they also serve as a tranquil view of eternity that serves to inspire our imaginations and stir the creativity in the soul.

We will make bold advances in science only when we dare to dream. The future is the final frontier. We must never stop our search.

T.S. Eliot may have put it best when he wrote:

"We shall not cease from exploration
And the end of our exploring
Will be to arrive where we started
And know the place for the first time."
—Alex Burleson

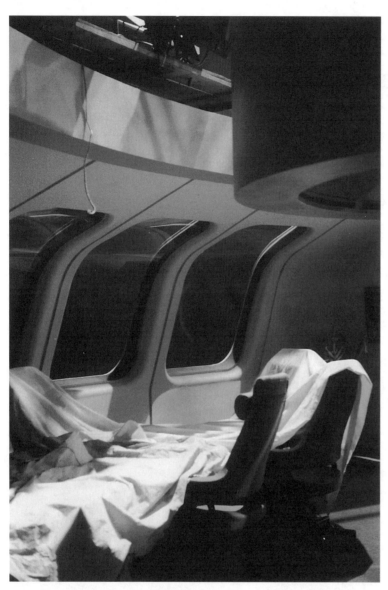

Observation Lounge from doorway leading to bridge.
Photo c 1994 "Deep Focus"

POETIC LICENSE AND THE TRANSPORTER AS DEUS EX MACHINA

The transporter has been an integral part of the STAR TREK universe since the show was created. But in spite of all it has been shown to be capable of, no one has ever really explained how it does all that it can seemingly do.

Deus Ex Machina (da-oos ex mak-ee-na) n. 1 (literally "God from the Machine") In Greek drama, a character portraying a deity, lowered to the stage by a largely unseen mechanism; the deity rights wrongs and presents the moral of the drama. 2 (informal) A dramatically unviable resolution to a conflict.

STAR TREK has its share of Gods from the Machine, and several episodes feature conflict resolutions in which the scriptwriter, having painted himself into a proverbial corner, falls back on pseudo-science (and poorly reasoned pseudo-science at that) for relief. No Trek technology has been abused more than that of the transporter, which has been called upon to act as deus ex machina more than any other device.

The transporter technology was envisioned by STAR TREK creator Gene Roddenberry as a

The Transporter Room   Photo c 1994 "Deep Fosuc"

method of moving dramatis personae from the Enterprise to a scene of action, i.e. a planet, a space station or another vessel, without having to slow an episode's dramatic progression with expensive and time consuming special effects sequences involving shuttlecraft launches and landings or docking maneuvers.

The theory behind the transporter is a stock science fiction concept and has been the technological impetus behind many other novels, short stories and films, most notably "The Fly" and its theatrical adaptation of the same title.

WHO REALLY KNOWS HOW IT WORKS?

As presented in the primary course material, the industrial ramifications of transporter technology are revolutionary. In "The Nth Degree" we see a crewman instruct the computer by verbal command to create complex, intricate equipment on the holodeck, a device that uses transporter technology, normally to create an atmosphere conducive to rest and recreation among the crew. The equipment created under these conditions is advanced enough to cause the Enterprise's Chief Engineer (surely one of the best engineering minds Starfleet has to offer, as he serves aboard the fleet's flagship) to admit that he doesn't actually understand how it functions. Furthermore, this maze of advanced equipment is created instantaneously.

The ramifications of the technology lie fallow. If the transporter/replicator system is capable of creating equipment more advanced than that currently in use by the Federation, it follows that it is easily capable of creating equipment as advanced as that currently in use. Starship construction, for instance, need not be a labor and time intensive industry; one person, instructing a replicator, could create a vessel in weeks, if not days. Unfortunately the series fails to deal with this aspect of the technology.

In "The Best of Both Worlds, Part II," the viewer is told that it will take Starfleet two years to recover from the devastating loss of nearly 40 starships at the battle of Wolf 359.

In the Classic Trek episode "Catspaw," Captain Kirk responds to a bribery offer of gemstones by claiming that the Enterprise is capable of manufacturing gems of the same quality in any quantity. This is consistent with Captain Picard's claim in "The Neutral Zone" that the Federation has done away with money and personal wealth.

THE TRANSPORTER AS CURE-ALL

Again, the effects of the technology on society are unexplored. Scarce resources limit population growth, for instance, as well as becoming the underlying reason behind almost all armed conflicts. With technology that can instantly recreate any resource in any amount, wars should be a thing of the past. Combined with the effects of the technology on living tissue (recounted below), overpopulation should be a rampant problem through the Federation, yet only the Classic Trek episode "Mark Of Gideon" dealt with overpopulation, and that took place on a non-Federation world.

Additionally, societies use wealth (and, usually, its attendant power and authority) as a way of rewarding exemplary performance in society's service and/or as a motivating factor to induce members of the population to take on undesirable tasks. If items such as gemstones and gold could be reproduced at will, wealth would cease to have meaning and it would be difficult at best to inspire individuals to strive for superior accomplishment or labor at a distasteful position.

The possible effects of the transporter technology on living tissue are also nothing short of revolutionary. Several episodes have portrayed the transporter as capable of curing illnesses by simply leaving the infecting or viral agent out of the re-integration process, for instance. In "Unnatural Selection," Dr. Kathryn Pulaski becomes infected with a bio-engineered virus which is removed from her body by having the transporter re-integrate her based on a pre-existing pattern obtained before the virus invaded her system (with the clear moral, "If you're about to go on a dangerous away team, brush your hair.").

SORTING IT ALL OUT

In the animated episode "The Terratine Incident," the Enterprise crew encounters radiation which causes spiral molecular chains (such as DNA molecules) to contract. The crew is shrinking rapidly until the idea is advanced to run them through the transporter, again using the re-integration process to return them to the state of their last transport. The animated series actually used the transporter twice to cure physiological disorders and originated the identical concept which was repeated with the transporter in THE NEXT GENERATION episode "Unnatural Selection."

Another set of episodes indicate that the transporter is capable of dealing with the mind and body as separate elements. In

"Lonely Among Us" Captain Picard, while sharing a symbiotic relationship with an alien, transports himself into space. His consciousness, along with that of the entity in symbiosis with him, joins with a colony of noncorporeal beings, but decides to return to the Enterprise. The crew is able to regenerate his no longer extant body (more on this later) and re-integrate his consciousness with it as a whole.

In the original series episode "Turnabout Intruder" Kirk's consciousness is forcibly exchanged with that of a woman who feels that her gender held her back from attaining a starship command; so she uses a transporter-like device to effect the change. In the aforementioned "Unnatural Selection," Pulaski's body is returned to its pre-virus state but, significantly, her memories of events after she was struck by the virus remain intact.

THE SECRET OF IMMORTALITY?

Finally, as depicted, the transporter technology is capable of controlling the aging process. To refer once again to "Unnatural Selection," the virus which attacks Pulaski causes rapid aging, reversed by using the transporter. In the animated "The Counter-Clock Incident," the Enterprise enters an alternate dimension in which time flow is reversed from our norm (as well as functioning on a more accelerated level). Once again the transporter comes to the rescue and the newly infantile crew are returned to their former selves.

All of these plots would be the stuff of good science fiction if their effects upon human culture were examined. Logically speaking, for instance, access to technology which can control aging among a race notoriously in fear of the process of death and dying should result in almost universal immortality. Similarly, the ability to sift the mind and body sepa-

The Transporter Room   Photo c 1994 "Deep Focus"

rately during the transport process would yield a culture in which very few persons deviated from the culture-bound norms of attractiveness. (Sex change operations would also become much simpler.) Finally, illness would literally be a thing of the past, as any pathological symptoms could be cured immediately by a transport.

Various arguments have been advanced by several episodes as well as by those who follow the series to explain these inconsistencies. Many episodes hint that the transporter-related replicator cannot completely and accurately replicate anything; foodstuffs from the replicator are said to have a certain "off" taste, for example. Since the transporter uses the same technology, and assuming that there is no difference in the scanning resolution of the transporter and the replicator, it seems odd that anyone would use the device at all if these were true as it would indicate that there was a reasonably high chance of being inaccurately re-integrated at the destination.

THE NAKED TRUTH

Other arguments have asserted that the transporter lacks fine enough control to be usable for industrial construction; the assembly of starships, for instance. Evidence in the series contradicts this point of view. The Classic

Trek episode "Tomorrow Is Yesterday" features a jet interceptor pilot being transported into the cockpit of his plane. In "Menage A Troi" the Ferengi use a transporter to beam Deanna and Lwaxana Troi out of their clothing, implying a molecular level registration. It's hard to get much finer control than that.

Further arguments have held that the device is incapable of altering the pattern of matter in transit. Again this goes against the trend of information imparted during the series. The previously mentioned episodes "The Terratin Incident" and "Lonely Among Us" both feature the creation of physical matter from inert mass or modification of physical matter from its initial pattern. In "The Enemy Within" Captain Kirk is split into two beings by the transporter, both of which have his original body mass, implying the ability of the transporter to create a physical form and an integrated source of inert matter for performing this operation. This concept was repeated in the NEXT GENERATION episode "Second Chances" in which a perfect duplicate of Will Riker was created which was even more identical than a clone would have been.

It is unfortunate that events such as these have taken place on a program which prides itself on believability and consistency, but perhaps it is also unavoidable. Writers have been utilizing the deus ex machina to solve their dramatic problems since the dawn of the dramatic form, and they will probably still be using it when the events portrayed in STAR TREK have come and gone.

—*David Gardner*

Michael Dorn at the Director's Guild premier of *Article 99*.
Photo c 1994 Albert L. Ortega

Brent Spiner at Paramount Studios with Marina Sirtis for the L.I.F.E. (Love is Feeding Everyone) project. Photo c 1994 Albert L. Ortega

MARINA SIRTIS ON QVC

Shopping channels have become increasingly popular on cable systems around the country, and the most imaginative one is QVC. They periodically bring on actors from the various STAR TREK series to entice fans into buying some special new collectible which is endorsed by one of their favorite performers. With the huge popularity of STAR TREK—THE NEXT GENERATION, actors from that cast have been making various appearances on the QVC shopping channel, including everyone's favorite Betazoid.

People don't spend enough money. They just plain don't buy enough, or so one would be led to believe by the proliferation of shopping channels. My cable system has three of them. The cable companies like them because they get them for free; since with the more basic cable systems to carry a shopping channel, the deeper is the pool of potential shoppers cruising down the information highway.

The shopping channel called QVC is perhaps the largest, and it's certainly the most imaginative. TV GUIDE lists the shopping categories the channel presents and one of those categories explored - on at least a bi-monthly basis - is STAR TREK. There are all kinds of Trek related goodies available to order, and many of them are quite interesting. But to draw those STAR TREK fans in, you need a personality. In December 1993 that STAR TREK personality was Marina Sirtis.

In spite of the seeming limitations of the format, QVC makes it all interesting by taking advantage of the fact that it's live. They do this by pairing up the STAR TREK guest with a host who tends to know his Trek and who can therefore ask interesting questions and get into the kind of Trek trivia and behind-the-scenes information which just doesn't come out during a ten minute interview on THE ARSENIO HALL SHOW.

Marina was on QVC for two hours (the usual time slot for their STAR TREK sales pitches), and she seemed to enjoy herself. She was certainly open to answer questions and more than willing to discuss the items being offered for sale to the fans. She also clearly liked talking about her character, since, now in the seventh season of STAR TREK— THE NEXT GENERA-TION, Deanna Troi was a much more interesting character to talk about.

ON GIVING DEANNA MORE DIMENSION

"Not to kind of diminish her at all, but she's not just decorative any more," the actress stated. "There was a time, do you remember, in the second and third season, where she was decorative! I used to feel like a potted palm on the bridge," she said, explaining how her character used to basically just stand around without really doing or contributing anything. "I was just there to add a bit of color.

"But now, ever since they made her a psychologist and gave her that kind of responsibility, and gave [Troi] her own office and then finally put her in a uniform, she's become a part of the crew much more. Last season we saw her on away teams. This is what blows me away— she's now the expert on Romulan technology! Me, who had never said a word of technobabble in my life. Now I have to learn technobabble, and I'll give you a little secret here. In an up and coming episode, I get promoted to Commander," Marina revealed, which of course did happen in the excellent episode "Lower Decks."

These programs on QVC are interesting to watch because the STAR TREK items they offer for sale aren't the average ones you normally see offered by mail and at conventions. Besides the autographed items, they had a communications badge which made a noise when pressed as well offering uncut sheets of STAR TREK bubblegum cards and a limited gold foil edition of the first issue of the DEEP SPACE NINE comic book.

Because these shows are live, fans are also able to call in and ask the guest

Marina Sirtis at Hotel Nikko with husband Michael Lamber where the cast of *The Next Generation* was being honored by Education First.

Photo c 1994 Albert L. Ortega

questions, although I suspect that they had to purchase something first before the operator would pass them down the line.

DIRECTING THE NEXT GENERATION

One fan who called in asked Marina if she'd be directing an episode of THE NEXT GENERATION during the final season, like some of her costars on the show had previously done. But she said that she'd been turned

Marina Sirtis at the Pasadena Civic Center for the 92 Technical Emmys where she was a presenter.
Photo c 1994 Albert L. Ortega

down, when she made the request. "I think my executive producer decided that I wasn't maybe totally committed to it or serious about it, because he did say no. And I must admit that I didn't go and slash my wrists or anything. I asked because I thought it might be a good way of learning more about the business. I have to admit my real love is acting, and I don't really ever see myself behind a camera. It's a lot of hard work. Directing is very hard work and then your face doesn't end up on the screen at the end of the day, so I don't really see the point of it, to be honest. So you'll see me in front of the camera much more.

"You will see Gates [McFadden] directing, however. She'll be the first woman on STAR TREK from the cast to direct."

Marina was also asked about THE NEXT GENERATION movie due in late 1994, and while she would only talk about it a little, the actress revealed that it was slated to have both the original STAR TREK cast as well as the cast of THE NEXT GENERATION. "At one point a couple of the characters from each generation meet, but that's all I can tell you."

Figurines of characters from THE NEXT GENERATION were also being offered for sale on the show, and when asked what it's like when she sees herself as a figurine, she replied, "It's almost like it's not you. It's a really weird feeling. You have to kind of detach yourself from it in a weird kind of way because it's not an exact likeness." That's because it is difficult to achieve a true likeness in such a small

toy, but they remarked on the fact that the figures of Geordi and Dr. McCoy did manage to actually capture the likenesses of LeVar Burton and DeForest Kelley. "These are really fabulous," Marina insisted enthusiastically, "and they really need to be in a glass case."

ON KISSING A KLINGON

Marina would consistently make interesting remarks, such as when she mentioned having an informal contest with Leonard Nimoy over who can sign the most autographs in the shortest space of time as she'd recently signed 1500 autographs in an hour and ten minutes, which she believed had surpassed Leonard's record.

She also made a very strange remark, which I can only imagine will come back to haunt her. When the subject of Deanna's relationship with Worf on the show was mentioned, she stated,

"When I misbehave, the producers find these kind of subtle and devious ways to punish me. So they kind of got me paired off with Worf right now in a couple of episodes. And he does insist on wearing those ugly teeth every time we have to kiss.

"Can you explain to me how you can get a kiss wrong? It's like every time we have to kiss, Michael Dorn is going, 'Cut! Cut! We've got to do it again!' And I'm going, 'I'm wearing my lips out, Michael.'"

Marina expressed undisguised respect for Classic Trek, and in fact when a caller referred to the earlier series as "old" STAR TREK she quickly corrected them and said that it must be called "original" STAR TREK.

The subject of season seven being the last year for the NEXT GENERATION came up, and Marina said that she'd been wailing ever since she heard that it would be the last season. "I'm very upset that it's the last year, but you know there's a movie to look forward to, so it's not like we're gone, and we're never coming back. We are going to be making the movies."

THE ORIGIN OF THE ACCENT

The host mentioned in passing Marina's Betazoid accent that she had made up for the series and it turned out that she was upset about something connected with that particular fact.

"What happens is they make up reasons for things after the fact," she explained. "So they had these Klingons that didn't look like Klingons, they looked like normal people with pointy ears, but they were just in a bad mood all the time, if I remember right. And then we have my accent.

"Now when I originally got the part, they said to me, okay, you can't be British because the captain's British, and he's far more important than you, is what they said basically. I said fine. I've always done accents in my career because I look dark.

Where do you want the accent to come from and they said Betazed. So I made up this accent; who's going to be able to tell me I'm doing it wrong? I basically made it up. But then we met mom, and mom was from the American sector of Betazed, you see, and so I went to the producers and said, so where is my accent from? And they said, oh, it's your father's accent. So I said okay, that would work.

"And then of course we met dad last year and he was from San Diego or somewhere like that. So I have no idea where my accent comes from! Consequently I've had to kind of Americanize it to make her kind of mid-Atlantic because it really does sound kind of strange that Troi talks funny. Things change and get reasons. I think the latest thing is that they sent me away to school, and that's why I talk with this funny accent."

THE FUTURE OF STAR TREK

The live interview with Marina was a good opportunity for people to ask questions about rumors and, therefore, get to the bottom of things. For instance, one caller stated that he'd heard that Marina had been signed on to the cast of the forthcoming STAR TREK spin-off, but she said that this was not true at all.

"No, that isn't true. I think they want a whole new crew for the show, which is going to be called VOYAGER. The idea is that the NEXT GENERATION cast will be off making movies. We did kind of drop hints," she admitted, suggesting that some of the TNG actors would really like to be on a new STAR TREK series. "Jonathan and I were going around saying that it was going to be called THE RIKERS IN SPACE, but that kind of fell on deaf ears I have to admit."

The host said that he could really get into that idea and suggested that it would open with Troi and Riker at the piano singing: "Boy the way the Klingons played. . ." which Marina thought was a very funny idea.

"We thought about a STAR TREK sitcom, which hadn't been done before, but the studio didn't buy it, so it's going to be a whole new group of people you will grow to love, I'm sure."

When the caller remarked that he looked forward to the NEXT GENERATION movies, Marina told him that he should see each one of them twenty times and take all of his family, too.

Jonathan Frakes at the February, 1990 March of Dimes honor for Gene Roddenberry with wife Genie, Michael Dorn and his date.   Photo c 1994 Albert L. Ortega

CAN WE TALK TREK?
THE NEXT GENERATION CAST
VISITS THE JOAN RIVERS SHOW

Perhaps to make up for his debacle with GOOD MORNING AMERICA, Patrick Stewart appeared with other cast members of NEXT GEN later that same year on this syndicated talk show, and a good time was had by all.

On November 16th, 1992, most of the regular cast of STAR TREK—THE NEXT GENERATION descended upon the set of THE JOAN RIVERS SHOW. As might be expected, this was pure showbiz, with the studio audience getting more of a buzz from the fame of the guests than any real information about them. This was not to be an interview of any great depth. It was more geared to the fast-paced and frothy style of the average daytime talk show. JOAN RIVERS was one of the only daytime talk shows to avoid having victims of society as her guests, choosing to usually go the more upscale route. It's unfortunate that her show has since been transmogrified into a silly shopping show.

But things were still going great back in '92 and on this day they got off to a rousing start by showing a clip from TNG episode "Birthright."

Then Joan Rivers introduced Stewart, who entered to the theme of THE NEXT GENERATION. This was a mawkish meeting, as Rivers gushed all over Stewart, referring to his work in I, CLAUDIUS and "A Christmas Carol."

"I should tell you," he joked, "that I am a much more unpleasant man than the one I played in I, CLAUDIUS." (Actually, his character there, one Sejanus, was one of the most wicked characters in that series, which was filled with wicked characters and very few pleasant ones.) Stewart then proceeded to flatter Rivers shamelessly; it was already obvious that this was going to be a program filled with repellent show-biz schmoozing.

After going on about the quality of the backstage hospitality, Stewart fielded questions about his classical acting and "A Christmas Carol." "It's not as much of a stretch as people imagine," he explained regarding his shift from Shakespeare to STAR TREK. "Sitting on that chair [the captain's chair] is something like sitting on the throne of England, only not quite as important. And so the transition was easy to make, as I've sat in a lot of thrones in my time."

Here the audience laughed, apparently due to the unintended double entendre meaning of the word throne as 'toilet.' Stewart continued: "When Marlon Brando came here, someone said to him, 'why did he give up the New York stage for Hollywood,' he said 'I didn't have the moral fiber to resist.' Well, part of that applies to me, too. It was too exciting to resist an American TV series for someone with my background."

After commenting on the recent presidential election, Stewart, obviously pleased with the results, admitted that he hadn't voted, but revealed that he was legally a resident alien, which prompted audience laughter at the double meaning of the word "alien." Needless to say, Rivers soon asked Stewart about the ongoing scandals of the British royal family. Stewart expressed sympathy for the royals and their private lives which are conducted in public view, and tied that in with Rivers' own tabloid troubles. Stewart himself had by this point been hit by the tabloids: "They wrote a lot of lies," he said, "and they quoted friends inappropriately, and they hurt my children; they made them unhappy and they made their friends unhappy. It was a miserable experience."

ENTER FRAKES & DORN

After a discussion of working with his son on STAR TREK—THE NEXT GENERATION, the program moved on and Rivers brought out Jonathan Frakes, preceded by a clip featuring Commander Riker.

Frakes discussed his long-distance relationship with his wife, since he and she work on opposite sides of the country. (They have a very large monthly phone bill.) He recounted that his first big break on stage was in a musical called "Shenandoah," a part he landed after a "cattle call," or general audition.

"Do you ever want to get your own ship?" asked Rivers.

"Not if it means giving up this job," replied Frakes. He then discussed the then-upcoming spin-off DEEP SPACE NINE, but only in the vaguest of terms beyond the fact that Patrick Stewart was going to be in it. Stewart went on to explain that DS9 would be a darker, bleaker, grittier show than THE NEXT GENERATION.

The third cast member to come out was Michael Dorn, after a clip showing Worf in a battle situation. (Note that Joan Rivers pronounces "Klingon" more as if it were spelled "Klingen.") Rivers asked typical questions: how long does the makeup take, et cetera, and Dorn trotted out the usual rote answers. But he did display some wit: when Rivers asks if he ever has any skin trouble from all the makeup he wears, he quipped, "Yes, they were going to send me to a leper colony for a while. It was really pretty bad for about two years. But they were really good about cutting the glue down and trying to not take so much time."

A CHANGE OF CHARACTER

After discussing Dorn's interest in flying—always bound to come up in the course of any interview, his rote human interest angle—the conversation turned to Dorn's earlier acting career, and hinged on one obvious aspect of it: prior to the role of Worf, Dorn always portrayed very nice characters: cops, doctors, all around good guys. This was why he jumped at the chance to portray the surly Klingon.

Then it came time for Marina Sirtis to join the cast on-stage (it's a little unclear what determined the order here, since it didn't seem to follow their ranks precisely). Out of character, Sirtis spoke in her charming London accent, an accent subdued on THE NEXT GENERATION. Sirtis revealed that she had been evacuated out of her house that morning; it seems that a neighbor had died, and it had been discovered that this neighbor had buried four cases of dynamite in her back yard! She had to buy a dress for her appearance on the Rivers show, and was worried about all the gifts she had received for her recent wedding. Typically, Rivers then pressed for details of Sirtis' personal life.

Next up was a clip of Dr. Crusher in action, followed by the entrance of Gates McFadden. McFadden discussed her new son and how she brings him to the set, where the rest of the cast takes care of him, but faltered on her own child's name; Patrick Stewart reminded her that the baby's name was, in fact, Jack. McFadden revealed that she had discovered her pregnancy the day she had last appeared on JOAN RIVERS, and joked that she was worried it might happen again. She then went on to recount how her pregnancy was concealed on the show: "Those lab coats just kept getting bigger every episode. It was like a ski parka, and finally, it was huge. I had one of my first big love episodes ever when I was seven months pregnant. I was big."

SPINER SPEAKS

The final guest was Brent Spiner. Again, a clip of him in character was shown from NEXT GEN-ERATION, followed by his entrance. Rivers started in by observing that Spiner's role of Data can't get older. (This was some time before a throwaway line in a seventh season episode revealed the previously-unknown fact that Data is programmed to age in appearance!) "What are they doing," asked Rivers, "and who is the doctor?"

"She's the doctor," replied Spiner, indicating

Gates McFadden, "it's just sort of a makeup thing. In my own life I am getting older, actually. I'm trying to avoid it, but I'm having no success."

"Do they have you watch your weight?"

"Weight isn't my prob-lem—age is."

When Rivers asked Spiner how he was able to play an emotionless android, he joked, "It's really not that difficult. This is an illusion, actually. I'm really a very emotion-less human being."

Rivers noted that Spiner had smiled once on the show.

"Oh—I smiled when I had sex."

"In the episode. . .?"

"Oh! In the episode!" This brought a round of laughter from the audience. Rivers then moved along to discuss Spiner's then-recent album of old standards, "Old Yellow Eyes Is Back," and Spiner's stage career, which included several successes and a major role in the ill-fated musical version of The Three Musketeers—the biggest money-losing show in Broadway history.

A ROUND TABLE INTERVIEW

After the next break, the discussion opened up to the whole cast (LeVar Burton was absent). Typical questions: who was a fan of STAR TREK before signing on to the show? Only Michael Dorn was, to any degree, and he claimed he could identify any classic Trek episode in the first thirty seconds—"when Kirk comes out and he's got a different wig on…"

A bit of over-reverent discussion of the late Gene Roddenberry ensued for a while; Spiner recounted oft-told Ray Bradbury's story about how he would sign autographs for people who mistook him for Roddenberry. Then, dredging for questions, Rivers asked the cast which century they would most like to visit on the show. Spiner chose the 20th cen-tury, as did Gates McFadden (if not ancient Greece) and Marina Sirtis. Michael Dorn was more specific: he wanted to go back to the 1940s and experience the aviation of that period. Jonathan Frakes chose the 1920s—"Trombone players did better in the Twenties," he explained.

Stewart expressed an interest in ancient Rome because the clothes of that period—togas—were so comfortable and loose-fitting. Basically, all were eager to get away from the 24th Century, where their jobs keep them up to eighteen hours a day. A brief discussion of 24th century sex, and of "spaceship acting"—the synchronized movement of the cast to simulate the ship's movement when hit by a phaser blast—rounded out the rest of the segment. Looking forward to moving into the motion pictures, the cast ended the mass interview on an upbeat note.

BRIEF AND LITTLE REMEMBERED

Despite the shortcomings of the above talk show appearance, it was brilliant when compared to Jonathan Frakes' appearance nearly a year later (September 28th, 1992) on the deservedly short-lived Chevy Chase show. After a lame comedy sketch about the changing of the guard at the "legendary Chevy Chase Theater," Chase, obviously bored, introduced Frakes with a clip and then exchanged pleasantries with the actor. Frakes was all right; the problem was with Chase, who hadn't researched his guest much, if at all.

"Why do you go to conventions?" he asked at one point.

"They pay," replied Frakes. "2000 screaming trekkies—some of them have turtles on their heads."

"Some have turtles in their heads," Chase quipped.

"Glad you said it. . ."

Matters didn't get much better. "Were you a trekkie fan yourself?" inquired Chase.

"I became one very fast," said Frakes.

"I mean for Shatner and Nimoy and those guys..."

"Who? "

After Chase spent some time rambling about the Vulcan hand sign, the two men talked about their wives and how they met in a fairly fragmented fashion that was relatively pointless, Chase bringing up UNDER THE RAINBOW in a strange reference to that early film of his. Then Chase brought up the subject of NEXT GENERATION movies.

"I've heard that rumor," said Frakes. "I think it's still a rumor."

"The STAR TREK pictures are great," opined Chase, "particularly the ones with Leonard and. . ."

"Believe me, they won't be in it."

Chase then went on to wonder why none of the old cast had been on THE NEXT GENERATION, since that would have been a good idea. Frakes explained that some of them had been on the show. This was the end of the segment. Chase, who obviously didn't care much about his own show

A Next Generation Celebration   123

or the background of his guests, demonstrated what a poor host he was. Perhaps he lacked even the most rudimentary research staff. The Joan Rivers appearance was frothy showbiz at best, but this was the ultimate nadir of any STAR TREK talk show appearance.

There are talk shows and then there are talk shows. After seeing the botched job Chevy Chase did, one started missing the parade of the damaged and the wounded who normally occupy the daytime guest slots. I guess it's true what they say—a talk show is only as good as its host because even a great guest can come off looking bad in a slovenly interview.

A model-in-progress of the Klingon engine room.   Photo c 1994 "Deep Focus"

A NEXT GENERATION TRIVIA CONTEST

The following are a list of questions followed by their answers. They have been arranged in an easy to access manner so that someone can either read the questions from the book, and have immediate access there to the answers, or else copy them and hold the answers back. The questions vary in difficulty from novice to—clearly—master level of Trek trivia.

PART A

In what episode. . . ?

1 Were Keiko and Miles married?
2 Did Captain Picard mention Khan Singh?
3 Was Wesley ordered executed?
4 Did Data create a holodeck comic?
5 Did O'Brien complain about sushi?
6 Did Guinan first mention a Tartazian Razorbeast?
7 Did Guinan next mention the beast?
8 Did Picard and Riker use the phaser range?

9 Did Guinan and Worf use the phaser range?

10 Did Alexander first use the holodeck?

ANSWERS PART A

1 Data's Day
2 A Matter of Time
3 Justice
4 The Outrageous Okona
5 The Wounded
6 Imaginary Friend
7 Rascals
8 A Matter of Honor
9 Redemption I
10 New Ground

PART B) SHIPS THAT PASS IN THE NIGHT

Which episode was the _____ mentioned in?

A USS Bozeman
B USS Yosemite
C USS Horatio
D USS Britaine
E USS Melbourne
F USS Hathaway
G USS Aries
H Klingon ship Bortas
I Klingon ship Kruge
J USS Tschikovsky
K USS Hood
L USS Victory
M USS Yamato
N USS Enterprise 1701-C
O USS Sutherland
P USS Excalibur
Q USS Phoenix
R USS Rutledge
S USS Tianamin
T Klingon ship Hectar
U USS Thomas Paine
V USS Renegade
W USS Fearless
X USS Ajax
Y Talarian ship Batress
Z USS Drak

ANSWERS TO PART B

A CAUSE AND EFFECT
B REALM OF FEAR
C CONSPIRACY
D NIGHT TERRORS
E BEST OF BOTH WORLDS I/II AND 11001001
F PEAK PERFORMANCE
G THE ICARUS FACTOR
H REDEMPTION I
I UNIFICATION I/II
J THE NAKED NOW
K TIN MAN AND ENCOUNTER AT FARPOINT
L ELEMENTARY, DEAR DATA
M CONTAGION AND WHERE SILENCE HAS LEASE
N YESTERDAY'S ENTERPRISE
O REDEMPTION I
P REDEMPTION II
Q THE WOUNDED
R THE WOUNDED
S REDEMPTION II
T REDEMPTION I/II
U CONSPIRACY
V CONSPIRACY

W WHERE NO ONE HAS GONE
   BE-FORE
X WHERE NO ONE HAS GONE
   BE-FORE
Y HEART OF GLORY
Z THE ARSENAL OF FREEDOM

PART C) BEYOND
MASTERS

1 What year did the United Nations rule that no Earth citizen could be tried for crimes of humanity?

2 What year did Q claim the Post Atomic Horror Court was set?

3 How many people died aboard S.S. Tschicovsky?

4 What planet did Lutan rule?

5 What disease could be cured by a vaccine on that planet?

6 When did the T'kon Empire die out?

7 What did the Ferengi steal in THE LAST OUTPOST?

8 Where did they steal it from?

9 What was the Portal's identification number?

10 On what Stardate was Wesley Crusher promoted to acting ensign?

ANSWERS TO PART C

1 2036
2 2079
3 80
4 Ligon II
5 Angalese Fever
6 600,000 years ago
7 A T-9 Energy Converter
8 Gamma Tauri IV
9 Number 63
10 41263.4

BONUS QUESTIONS:

A) What is Dixon Hill's phone number?

B) How many colonists does Data hold the knowledge of?

C) In WHEN THE BOUGH BREAKS, Harry says he used to live on...?

D) What was the ambassador being held hostage in TOO SHORT A SEASON named?

E) How many hostages did Jameson free 45 years previously?

F) Name the two Benzite characters from COMING OF AGE and A MATTER OF HONOR.

G) What race of web-fingered humanoids disdains courtesy?

H) What kind of weapons system threatened the Enterprise in THE ARSENAL OF FREEDOM?

BONUS ANSWERS:

A   Prospect 4631
B   411
C   Zeta IV
D   Ambassador Hawkins
E   63
F   Mordock and Mendon
G   The Zoldon
H   An Echo Popper 607

MASTER TRIVIA

QUESTIONS:

IDENTIFY EPISODE COMMONALTY

1 In what two sixth season episodes do we hear excerpts of Data's poem "Ode To Spot"?

2 In what fifth and sixth season episodes does Guinan mention a Tartazian Razor Beast?

3 What was the NEXT GEN episode that introduced the wicked Cardassians into the STAR TREK universe and the episode with the next spoken reference of a Cardassian freighter?

NUMBERS, NUMBERS, NUMBERS:

4) What is Captain Jean-Luc Picard's serial number?

5) What is the USS STARGAZER's registration number?

6) What is Yeoman Janice Rand's original cabin number?

7) What did Kevin Neelan's TREKKIE character in the SAT. NIGHT LIVE "GET A LIFE" sketch claim her cabin number was?

MOTHER'S NAMES:

8) What is Spock's mother's maiden name?

9) What is Kirk's mother's first name?

IMZADI:

10) What ship did Lt. Riker serve as second officer on when he arrived on Betazed to first meet Troi?

11) What ship did Lt. Riker leave Betazed as first officer of?

12) What is William T. Riker's middle name?

FIRST DEEP SPACE NINE TRIVIA:

13) What village does Keiko's mother live in?

14) What ship did Ben Sisko serve on at Wolf 359

15) What planet did the captain of that ship come from?

16) In the very first scene of DS9, what is the name of the first starship seen destroyed by the Borg?

17) What was the name of the runabout starship that Ben and Dax used to first penetrate the wormhole?

18) How did Chief Operations Officer O'Brien manage to get Odo off the Cardassian ship when the transporter wouldn't energize?

19) How many lemonades was Ben carrying on Gilgo Beach?

20) How many millennia did Bajoran monks study the orbs?

BONUS: What is Pavel Chekov's middle name?

MASTER TRIVIA ANSWERS:

1) SCHISMS and A FISTFUL OF DATAS

2) IMAGINARY FRIEND and RASCALS

3) THE WOUNDED and THE MIND'S EYE

4) SP-937-215 (CHAIN OF COMMAND)

5) NCC-2893 (THE BATTLE)

6) 3C 46 (Classic Trek: BLOOPER REEL NUMBER ONE)

7) Y-390 (SNL - GET A LIFE!)

8) Amanda Grayson (Classic novel - STRANGERS FROM THE SKY)

9) Winona (Classic novels - MEMORY PRIME/TIME FOR YESTERDAY)

10) The science exploration vessel FORTUNA (TNG novel - IMZADI)

11) The USS HOOD (ENCOUNTER AT FARPOINT/TNG NOVEL - IMZADI)

12) Thelonius (TNG novel - IMZADI)

13) Komamoto (DS9 - THE EMISSARY)

14) USS SARATOGA (DS9 - THE EMISSARY)

15) Vulcan - 40 Eridani A-1 (DS9 - THE EMISSARY/ STARFLEET DYNAMICS)

16) USS MELBOURNE (DS9 - THE EMISSARY)

17) RIO GRANDE (DS9 - THE EMISSARY)

18) He kicked it (DS9 - THE EMISSARY)

19) Three (DS9 - THE EMISSARY)

20) Ten (DS9 - THE EMISSARY)

BONUS: Alexandrovitch (Classic novel - HOME IS THE HUNTER)

TREK TRIVIA BY EPISODE

ENCOUNTER AT FARPOINT

1 What planet was Farpoint Station located on?

Answer: (Deneb IV)

2 What race populated that planet?

Answer: (The Bandi)

3 Who was the leader of the natives?

Answer: (Groppler Zorn)

4 What bridge officer was frozen solid on the bridge?

Answer: (Lt. Torres)

5 What bridge officer was frozen in a courtroom?

Answer: (Tasha Yar)

6 What was the first death scene on NEXT GEN?

Answer: (A bailiff is machine-gunned to death)

7 How is his body disposed of?

Answer: (Dragged off by chain on leg)

8 What Terran group proclaimed no Earth resident could be held libel for the crimes of his race?

Answer: (New United Nations)

9 What year did that law go into effect?

Answer: (2036)

10 What year did Q claim the court to be set in?

Answer: (2079)

11 Who was the first person to be seen enveloped by a transporter beam?

Answer: (Riker)

12 What ship did Beverly and Wes ride to Farpoint Station on?

Answer: (USS HOOD)

13 What two new Enterprise officers served on that ship?

Answer: (Riker/LaForge)

14 Who is the first person to greet Riker on arrival?

Answer: (Yar)

15 What three characters appear in red shirts, who later switch to gold uniform shirts the following year?

Answer: (Geordi/O'Brien/Worf)

16 What planet did Riker attempt to keep the HOOD's captain from beaming down to?

Answer: (Altair III)

17 What was the captain's name?

Answer: (DeSoto)

18 In what future episode is that captain first seen?

Answer: (TIN MAN)

19) In what future episode is the HOOD referred to?

Answer: (ALLEGIANCE)

20 What message does Picard send the captain?

Answer: (Bon voyage, mon amie)

21 When does Picard finally compliment Riker for the docking procedure he performs?

Answer: (THE ICARUS FACTOR)\

22 What costumes did Q appear in?

Answer: (17th century Elizabethan Captain, 20th century US Marine Captain, 21st century Fourth World Mercenaries' Captain and a 21st century judge.)

23 What action did Picard ask Worf if he intended to take, when Q appeared on the viewscreen?

Answer: (He asked if Worf planned to black a hole in the viewer)

24 What section of Shakespeare was first used on NEXT GEN?

Answer: (Henry IV: II - "Kill all the lawyers.")

25 Who uses that line?

Answer: (Picard)

26 How old is the "Admiral"?

Answer: (137 years old)

27 How does Worf describe the distinguished visitor from another generation?

Answer: ("A remarkable man.")

28 What race does he suggest Data belongs to?

Answer: (Vulcan)

29 Except for what feature?

Answer: ("I don't see no points on those ears, boy.")

30 What is unusual about the first scene of the Enterprise in orbit around a planet?

Answer: (The saucer section is missing.)

31 Who is in command of the saucer section?

Answer: (Worf)

32 What two former lovers are reunited on the bridge crew?

Answer: (Troi/Riker)

33 What special name do they have for each other?

Answer: (Imzadi)

34 How does that translate into Standard?

Answer: (Beloved)

THE NOVEL: ENCOUNTER AT FARPOINT

35 What admiral assigned the Enterprise to investigate?

Answer: (Admiral Hidalgo)

36 When did Picard stop receiving "motherly and fatherly" advice?

Answer: (Not since his 40th birthday)

37 How long did Beverly have her private practice?

Answer: (Eight years)

38 How long had she been in Starfleet at this time?

Answer: (15 years)

39 How old was Picard at Farpoint

Station?

Answer: (55)

40 What did Picard quote James T. Kirk has having said about being captain of the Enterprise?

Answer: (It was like "making love in a fishbowl.")

41 How old was Riker at Farpoint Station?

Answer: (32)

42 What did Ensign Mar Hughes refer to Picard as?

Answer: (An old burrhog)

43 Geordi's visual device is called a VISOR. What words do the letters VISOR represent?

Answer: (Visual Instrument and Sight Organ Replacement)

44 What position did LaForge serve at on the HOOD?

Answer: (Conn)

45 Where did Riker first meet Dr. Crusher?

Answer: (On the HOOD's trip to Farpoint Station)

46 Who held the all-time record for starship docking in the Starfleet Academy simulator?

Answer: (Riker)

47 What ship did Riker serve on before becoming first officer on the HOOD?

Answer: (The Yorktown)

48 What was his position on that ship?

Answer: (Second officer)

49 How long did he serve on that ship?

Answer: (3 years)

50 Why did Admiral McCoy miss the launch of the Enterprise-D?

Answer: (He was in Bethesda Starfleet Hospital)

51 For what reason was he admitted?

Answer: (broke his knee ligaments)

52 How did he injure himself?

Answer: (tripped over great-great grand-children's toys on his way to see the Enterprise-D launched)

53 Where did the Enterprise launch from?

Answer: (Mars spacedock)

54 What position did the admiral hold with Starfleet?

Answer: (Commander of Starfleet Medical Corps)

55 At what age did he retire?

Answer: (127 years)

56 Where did he retire to?

Answer: (A farm in Georgia)

57 What does the admiral like best about the new Enterprise?

Answer: (her name)

58 Who piped Picard aboard the Enterprise?

Answer: (Data)

59 How long into STARGAZER's mission was Jack Crusher killed?

Answer: (3 months)

60 According to the novel, ENCOUNTER AT FARPOINT, how did Jack Crusher die?

Answer: (He was killed when an away team was attacked by armed natives.)

61 How did Picard recover his body?

Answer: (At great risk, he personally retrieved the body)

62 How does this differ from the NEXT GEN novel, REUNION?

Answer: (In that novel, Jack dies from radiation while attempting to jettison a damaged nacelle on the STARGAZER.)

63 How does Picard's role differ?

Answer: (He attempts to save Jack, but instead decides to save closer crewmen. He would have died if he had attempted to reach Jack.)

64 In what NEXT GEN episode is Jack Crusher first seen?

Answer: (FAMILY)

65 What other episode does he appear in?

Answer: (VIOLATIONS)

66 What actor plays the late officer?

Answer: (Doug Wert)

67 Where does the "to boldly go where no one has gone before" line appear in the novel?

Answer: (It is Picard's first entry in his Captain's Log)

Answer: (It echoes initial entries of Robert April (FINAL FRONTIER), and James T. Kirk (ENTERPRISE.)

68 How does the crew respond in EAF novelization?

Answer: (They break into applause.)

69 What is Picard's response?

Answer: (Wait until we have something to applaud.)

70 In which two episodes does the bridge crew applaud Picard?

Answer: (THE BIG GOODBYE/SAMARITAN SNARE)

71 What line of dialogue did Picard interrupt Wesley?

Answer: ("High-resolution multi-fiber optic system-")

CODE OF HONOR

1 What planet is the Enterprise sent to recover a vaccine from? Answer: (Legon II)

2 What martial art does Tasha demonstrate for the aliens?

Answer: (Akido)

3 How does Data infuriate the captain?

Answer: (He refers to French as an 'obscure' language)

4 How does Picard respond?

Answer: (He informs Data that for years it was the language of civilization)

5 What unusual request does Bev make of Picard?

Answer: (She asks he allow Wes on the bridge)

6 How does Picard respond?

Answer: (He asks Wes to serve at Ops)

7 Where is the plague that the vaccine is needed for?

Answer: (Cyrus IV)

8 How many were projected to die?

Answer: (Millions)

9 What Starbase contacted the ENTERPRISE?

Answer: (Starbase 14)

10 Answer: What grooming activity does Geordi describe as an art form?

Answer: (Shaving)

THE NAKED NOW

1 What CLASSIC TREK character is mentioned for the first time?

Answer: (Captain James T. Kirk)

2 In what context was the character mentioned?

Answer: (Picard noted-in-passing while finding similarities between the two incidents)

3 What commonalty convinced Riker of a connection?

Answer: (A person taking a shower with their clothes on)

4 Who commandeers Main Engineering?

Answer: (Wesley Crusher)

5 How does he keep control?

Answer: (A repulsor beam)

6 How did the bridge crew on the other ship die?

Answer: (They blew the emergency hatch)

7 How did Riker describe the event?

Answer: (They were sucked out into space)

8 How did Data correct him?

Answer: (That's blown out, sir.)

9 Who was the first affected on the ENTERPRISE?

Answer: (Geordi)

10 Who did he pass it on to?

Answer: (Tasha)

11 Who did she then infect?

Answer: (Troi/Data)

12 Which two members of the bridge crew had sex?

Answer: (Tasha/Data)

13 Which four members considered it?

Answer: (Beverly/Picard, Riker/Troi)

14 Who saved the ship at the last second?

Answer: (Wesley and Data)

15 How did Wes distract engineers?

Answer: (Tape of Picard's voice)

16 How did Data compare himself to humans?

Answer: (Do we not both leak?)

WHERE NO ONE HAS GONE BEFORE

1 What vessel did the efficiency expert and his assistant arrive on?

Answer: (USS FEARLESS)

2 What other ship had they previously worked on?

Answer: (USS AJAX)

3 What was the expert's name?

Answer: (Kozinski)

4 Where did the ENTERPRISE wind up after the first test?

Answer: (Beyond Galaxy M-33)

5 How far did they travel in light-years?

Answer: (Two million seven hundred thousand light years)

6 How long would it take to get home?

Answer: (Nearly three hundred years)

7 How long would it take to send a sub-space message?

Answer: (Fifty-one years, 10 months, 9 weeks, 16 days...)

8 On the first test, how fast did they accelerate?

Answer: ("Passing Warp 10. . . off the scale")

9 One the second test how fast did they travel?

Answer: ("Never left Warp 1.5")

10 How did Data describe the test?

Answer: ("Where none have gone before")

11 How far was the ENTERPRISE from the Milky Way Galaxy after the second test?

Answer: ("I billion light-years from our galaxy.")

12 What did the Traveler chastise Wesley for figuring out?

Answer: (That time/space and thought are interconnected)

13 Who does the Traveler compare Wesley to?

Answer: (Mozart)

14 What science did he recommend for the boy?

Answer: (time-energy propulsion)

15 What planet does the Traveler come from?

Answer: (Tau Alpha-C)

16 In what future episode does the Traveler reappear?

Answer: (REMEMBER ME)

17 What civilian is given a field-commission?

Answer: (Wesley Crusher is named Acting Ensign.)

18 What thought did Worf make appear on the bridge?

Answer: (His pet Targ)

19 What was his name?

Answer: (Do Home)

20 What animal did Tasha compare it to?

Answer: (A kitty-cat)

21 What happened to Tasha, after the cat triggered a nightmare?

Answer: (She imagined herself back on her homeworld, pursued by a rape-gang)

22 What happens to Picard on the turbo-lift?

Answer: (He imagines he is stepping into warp space)

23 What does Chief Engineer Argyle propose to replace the warp barrier?

Answer: (The Kozinski Scale)

24 What color tutu was the ensign doing ballet wearing?

Answer: (Yellow)

25 What gibberish did the expert use to describe his work?

Answer: (Asymptomatically controlling tilling and vestal functions)

26 What is the next time such "faux" TREKSPEAK is used?

Answer: (RASCALS)

27 Who does Picard encounter in the hallway?

Answer: (His late mother)

28 Who interrupts his conversation with her?

Answer: (Riker)

29 Who did Picard say spoke like a true Academy graduate?

Answer: (Data)

30 What did Picard's mother offer him?

Answer: (Hot tea)

HAVEN

1 What hologram projection is Riker called away from?

Answer: (Two women in togas playing lyres)

2 Who would go naked in the planned wedding?

Answer: (Troi/Wyatt/Lwaxana/Stephen Miller)

3 How many times does Deanna kiss Wyatt?

Answer: (Twice)

4 What is the elected leader of Haven's title?

Answer: (Electarine)

5 What is her name?

Answer: (Valeda Innis)

6 What ship poses a threat to Haven?

Answer: (A Tarellian Plague ship)

7 How many survivors are on board when it contacts ENTERPRISE?

Answer: (Eight)

8 Who was Mr. Homm's predecessor as valet for Lwaxanna?

Answer: (Mr. Zilo)

9 Why was he fired?

Answer: (His thoughts about Lwaxana)

10 Where did Deanna get her accent?

Answer: (From her father)

11 Who did Lwaxana find to help break her of the accent?

Answer: (Mr. Zilo)

12 Robert Ellenstein played Stephen Miller. What role did he have in a STAR TREK film?

Answer: (He was the Federation president in ST IV: The Voyage Home.)

13 What caused the plague that wiped out the race?

Answer: (Biological warfare)

14 Where did Geordi say he heard of the case?

Answer: (Starfleet Academy)

15 What is the name of the infected race?

Answer: (The Terellians)

16 What is Lwaxanna's complete title?

Answer: (Daughter of the Fifth House, Holder of the Sacred Chalice of Riix, Heir to the Holy Rings of Betazed.)

17 What is the only line of dialogue Mr. Homm utters?

Answer: (Thank you for the drinks.)

18 When was the last alien believed to have died?

Answer: (Eight years ago.)

19 Who destroyed the survivors at that time?

Answer: (The Arsians)

20 Who refuses to toast Deanna's engagement?

Answer: (Riker)

21 What is the name of the woman who captures Wyatt's heart?

Answer: (Arianna)

22 What was the alien captain's name?

Answer: (Captain Wrenn)

23 What STAR TREK actor played the "dowry box"?

Answer: (Armin Shimerman)

24 Which two episodes did he appear as a Ferengi ?

Answer: (THE LAST OUTPOST/PEAK PERFORMANCE)

25 What regular role does the actor now have in DEEP SPACE NINE?

Answer: Quark)

TOO SHORT A SEASON

1 What is the name of the Admiral called back to service?

Answer: (Mark Jamison)

2 What happens to him over the course of the episode?

Answer: (He grows younger)

3 What two members of the bridge crew use a phaser to cut a hole in a wall on the planet?

Answer: (Tasha/Worf)

4 What name does the admiral call the ruler to convince him of his identity?

Answer: (Peritor)

5 What planet does the ENTERPRISE pick the admiral up from?

Answer: (Percifany 5)

6 What malady was the admiral suffering from?

Answer: (Iverson's Disease)

7 What was the name of the man who lured the admiral there?

Answer: (Karnus)

8 What planet did he lure him to?

Answer: (Mordan IV)

9 How long had that planet been fighting a civil war?

Answer: (40 years)

10 How long had it been since the war ended?

Answer: (5 years)

11 What planet were the advisors held hostage from?

Answer: (Cannos III)

12 Who first tells the bridge crew to "Make it so"?

Answer: (Admiral Jamison)

13 What was his wife's name?

Answer: (Anna)

14 Who did the admiral select for his away team?

Answer:
(Worf/Geordi/Data/Tasha/Jamison)

15 Who insisted on accompanying the away team?

Answer: (Picard)

16 Who risks his own life to save the admiral?

Answer: (Worf)

17 What are the admiral's last words?

Answer: ("I see only the gold")

18 Where did the admiral acquire the drug he used?

Answer: (Cervus II)

19 Why did they supply him with it?

Answer: (He negotiated a treaty for them)

20 How long did they supply him with it?

Answer: (2 years)

21 How many days did the ENTERPRISE have to deliver the admiral?

Answer: (6 days)

22 How many versions of the admiral's

photograph did Picard show the ruler?

Answer: (Three)

23 Why did the ruler want revenge on the admiral?

Answer: (For giving his opponents weapons, as well)

24 How did the ruler justify the war?

Answer: (Revenge for his father's death)

25 Who did the ruler believe ordered the assassination of his father?

Answer: (Old Patrice)

26 Who were the ruler's collaborators?

Answer: (Artimus/Gilmor)

27 What time-table did the ruler set for execution?

Answer: (1st - 5 min/ 1 - each 15 min)

28 How long had the admiral and his wife been married?

Answer: (One week short of their 50th anniversary)

29 How many hostages did Picard secure the release of?

Answer: (Twenty)

30 How many hostages did the admiral secure the release of?

Answer: (Sixty-three)

31 How many deaths did the admiral blame those lives on?

Answer: (Millions)

32 How did the admiral finally convince the ruler?

Answer: (A "v" shaped scar on his right forearm)

33 How long did the admiral expect the war to last?

Answer: (Less than a year)

REMEMBER ME

1 What Starbase was the ENTERPRISE stopping at?

Answer: (Starbase 133)

2 Whose log was read in the opening seconds?

Answer: (Chief Medical Officer's)

3 How do you spell the last name of Beverly's mentor?

Answer: (QUAICE)

4 What is his entire name?

Answer: (Dr. Daylon Quaice)

5 What was the name of the mentor's late wife?

Answer: (Patricia)

6 How long had the mentor served at that Starbase?

Answer: (6 years)

7 Where was the ENTERPRISE taking the mentor to?

Answer: (Kenda II)

8 Why was he returning there?

Answer: (It was his homeworld)

9 Where did Beverly first meet her mentor?

Answer: (Delos IV)

10 How did she meet him?

Answer: (She interned with him)

11 What room number did the mentor disappear from?

Answer: (Room 937)

12 What time did the mentor arrive on the ship?

Answer: (1600 hours)

13 What character that first appeared in SCHIZOID MAN is referred to?

Answer: (Dr. Selar)

14 How is she referred to?

Answer: (Missing)

15 What other episode is she also mentioned in?

Answer: (YESTERDAY'S ENTERPRISE)

16 What other role did the actress who portrayed the Vulcan doctor also appear on NEXT GEN?

Answer: (K'Ehleyr)

17 What episodes did that character appear in?

Answer: (THE EMISSARY/ REUNION)

18 What actress portrays both roles?

(Suzie Plakson)

19 What other doctor is reported missing along with the Vulcan?

Answer: (Dr. Hill)

20 Where did Picard tell Data to set a course for?

Answer: (Durinia IV)

21 When Beverly first asked how many people were on board, what was the stunning reply?

Answer: (230 crewmen in ship's compliment)

22 When Beverly next asked, how many were there?

Answer: (114 people)

23 Who were the last two left on board?

Answer: (Beverly/Jean-Luc)

24 In what order does Beverly list the missing bridge crew?

Answer: (Riker/ Troi/ Data/ O'Brien/ Geordi/ Worf/ Wesley/ my son)

25 What type of screen was Wes using to perform his warp bubble experiment?

Answer: (Subspace field geometry)

26 Which decks first suffer explosive decompression?

Answer: (Decks 5-14)

27 Followed by?

Answer: (Decks 3-15)

28 How large does the computer tell Beverly the universe is?

Answer: (705 meters in diameter)

29 What twentieth century motion picture does Bev refer to?

Answer: (The Wizard of Oz)

30 How did she refer to it?

Answer: (Just click my heels three times and I'm back in Kansas)

31 What other episode also referred to that work?

Answer: (THE SCHIZOID MAN)

32 What connection?

Answer: (Ira Graves whistled "If I Only Had A Heart")

33 How long would it take for the ENTERPRISE to reach the Traveler's home planet of Tau Alpha C at Warp 9.5?

Answer: (123 days)

34 What member of the bridge crew first disappears?

Answer: (Worf)

35 What does Beverly call him when she realizes they don't remember the fellow officer?

Answer: (The Big Guy. Never smiles. THE KLINGON!)

36 What is the minimum number of doctors normally on duty at all times?

Answer: (Four)

37 What is the name of the Federation ship that responded to Data's request for information?

Answer: (USS WELLINGTON)

38 What other ship also responded?

Answer: (A Ferengi vessel)

39 What was Picard's vital sighs on the bridge?

Answer: (Temp 37.2/Blood pressure 122/76/ Synaptic response 140/ Pulse 81/ Respiration 72)

40 Whose character's parent does Beverly mention?

Answer: (Troi's mother)

41 What musical instrument does Beverly mention?

Answer: (Trombone)

42 What efficiency expert from WHERE NO ONE HAS GONE BEFORE is referred to?

Answer: (Kozinski)

43 What character from that episode reappears?

Answer: (The Traveler)

44 What card game and form of music does Bev attribute to Riker?

Answer: (Poker and Jazz)

45 What does Bev say Deanna loves?

Answer: (Chocolate)

46 Who does Beverly accuse of never getting a punch line to a joke?

Answer: (Data)

47 When Beverly returns to the ENTERPRISE, how many are there?

Answer: (1,014)

STAR TREK: THE NEXT GENERATION ACTOR LIST

TNG Main Characters

PATRICK STEWART

(TNG - Captain Jean-Luc Picard)
(Locutus of Borg - TNG: THE BEST OF
BOTH WORLDS I/II)
(Director: IN THEORY/HERO WORSHIP/A
FISTFUL OF DATAS/PHANTASMS)

JONATHAN FRAKES

(TNG - Commander William Thomas Riker)
("Thomas" Riker - TNG: SECOND
CHANCES)
(Director: THE OFFSPRING/THE DRUM-
HEAD/CAUSE AND EFFECT/ THE QUALITY
OF LIFE/THE CHASE/ATTACHED/SUB
ROSA)

BRENT SPINER

(TNG - Commander Data)
(Lore - TNG: DATALORE/BROTHERS/
DESCENT I AND II)
(Dr. Noonian Soong - TNG:
BROTHERS/BIRTHRIGHT I)

MARINA SIRTIS

(TNG - Counselor Deanna Troi)
(Not in 11001001/HEART OF GLORY/HIDE AND Q/SYMBIOSIS)

LEVAR BURTON

(TNG - Lt. Commander Geordi LaForge)
(Director: SECOND CHANCES/THE PEGASUS)

MICHAEL DORN

(TNG - Lt. Worf)
(Colonel Worf - ST VI: The Undiscovered Country)

GATES MCFADDEN

(Dr. Beverly Crusher - TNG - all but second season)
(Did not appear in TNG: THE CHILD/WHERE SILENCE HAS LEASE/ ELEMENTARY, DEAR DATA/THE SCHIZOID MAN/ UNNATURAL SELECTION/A MATTER OF HONOR/THE MEASURE OF A MAN/THE DAUPHIN/CONTAGION/THE ROYALE/TIME SQUARED/THE ICARUS FACTOR/PEN PALS/ SAMARITAN SNARE/UP THE LONG LADDER/MANHUNT/THE EMISSARY/PEAK PERFORMANCE/SHADES OF GREY)
(Director: GENESIS)

WIL WHEATON

(Ensign Wesley Crusher - TNG)
(Cadet Wesley Crusher - TNG: THE GAME/THE FIRST DUTY)
(Alternate Wesley Crusher in TNG: PARALLELS)
(Adult Wesley Crusher was played by William A. Wallace in HIDE AND Q)

COLM MEANEY

(Battle Bridge Conn - TNG: ENCOUNTER AT FARPOINT I/II)
(Security - TNG: LONELY AMONG US)
(Transporter Chief - TNG: THE CHILD/WHERE SILENCE HAS LEASE/LOUD AS A WHISPER)\
(Chief Miles Edward O'Brien - TNG: UNNATURAL SELECTION/A MATTER OF HONOR/THE MEASURE OF A MAN/THE DAUPHIN/CONTAGION/TIME SQUARED/THE ICARUS FACTOR/PEN PALS/Q WHO?/UP THE LONG LADDER/MANHUNT/THE EMISSARY/SHADES OF GREY/THE ENSIGNS OF COMMAND/THE BONDING/BOOBY TRAP/THE ENEMY/THE PRICE/THE HUNTED/A MATTER OF PERSPECTIVE/THE MOST TOYS/BEST OF BOTH WORLDS I AND II/FAMILY/BROTHERS/DATA'S DAY/THE WOUNDED/CLUES/NIGHT TERRORS/HALF A LIFE/THE MIND'S EYE/IN THEORY/REDEMPTION I AND II/DARMOK/DISASTER/THE GAME/POWER PLAY/REALM OF FEAR/RELICS/RASCALS)
(DEEP SPACE NINE - Chief of Operations Miles Edward O'Brien)

WHOOPI GOLDBERG

(Guinan - TNG: THE CHILD/THE OUTRAGEOUS OKONA/THE MEASURE OF A MAN/THE DAUPHIN/Q WHO?/EVOLUTION/BOOBY TRAP/DEJA Q/YESTERDAY'S ENTERPRISE/THE OFFSPRING/BEST OF BOTH WORLDS I AND II/FAMILY/THE LOSS/CLUES/GALAXY'S CHILD/NIGHT TERRORS/RASCALS/SUSPICIONS)

ROSALIND CHAO

(Keiko Ishikawa O'Brien - TNG: DATA'S DAY/THE WOUNDED/NIGHT TERRORS/IN THEORY/DISASTER/VIOLATIONS/POWER PLAY/RASCALS)
(DS9 - A MAN ALONE/ IF WISHES WERE HORSES/ IN THE HANDS OF THE PROPHETS/THE SIEGE/ CARDASSIANS/ ARMAGEDDON GAME)

MICHELLE FORBES

(Ensign Ro Laren - TNG: ENSIGN RO/ DISASTER/ CONUNDRUM/ POWER PLAY/ CAUSE AND EFFECT/ THE NEXT PHASE/ RASCALS)
(Dora - TNG: HALF A LIFE)

DENISE CROSBY

(Security Chief Tasha Yar - TNG episodes 1-22)
(ENCOUNTER AT FARPOINT to SKIN OF EVIL)

(Alternate Tasha Yar - TNG: YESTERDAY'S ENTERPRISE)
(Sela - TNG: THE MIND'S EYES/ REDEMPTION I AND II/ UNIFICATION I AND II)

DIANA MULDAUR

(Dr. Katherine Polaski - TNG: THE CHILD/ WHERE SILENCE HAS LEASE/ ELEMENTARY, DEAR DATA/ THE SCHIZOID MAN/ UNNATURAL SELECTION/ A MATTER OF HONOR/ THE MEASURE OF A MAN/ THE DAUPHIN/ CONTAGION/ THE ROYALE/ TIME SQUARED/ THE ICARUS FACTOR/ PEN PALS/ SAMARITAN SNARE/ UP THE LONG LADDER/ MANHUNT/ THE EMISSARY/ PEAK PERFORMANCE/ SHADES O GREY)
(Dr. Anne Mulhall/Thalessa - CLASSIC TREK: RETURN TO TOMORROW)
(Dr. Miranda Jones - CLASSIC TREK: IS THERE IN TRUTH NO BEAUTY?)

MULTIPLE TNG APPEARANCES AS DIFFERENT CHARACTERS

MARC ALAIMO
(Antican Delegate - TNG: LONELY AMONG US, DS9: COMPANION)
(Romulan Commander T'Bok - TNG: THE NEUTRAL ZONE)
(Cardassian Gul Macet - TNG: THE WOUNDED)

(1880's Gambler - TNG: TIME'S ARROW)

(Gul Dukat - DS9: EMISSARY I-II/DUET/ THE HOMECOMING/ CARDASSIANS/ NECESSARY EVIL)

GARY ARMAGNAL
(Holodeck Dan Hill - TNG: THE BIG GOODBYE)

(1880's Policeman - TNG: TIME'S ARROW II)

CHRISTOPHER COLLINS
(Klingon Captain Kargon - TNG: A MATTER OF HONOR)

(Pakled Captain Grebnedlog - TNG: SAMARITAN SNARE)

FRANK CORSENTINO
(DaiMon Bok - TNG: THE BATTLE)

(DaiMon Tog - TNG: MENAGE A TROI)

DENISE CROSBY
(TNG - Security Chief Tasha Yar, episodes 1-22)

(Alternate Tasha Yar - TNG: YESTERDAY'S ENTERPRISE)

(Sela - TNG: THE MIND'S EYE/ REDEMPTION I-II/ UNIFICATION I-II)

MAX GRODENCHIK
(Sovak - TNG: CAPTAIN'S HOLIDAY)

(Par Lenor - TNG: THE PERFECT MATE)

(DS9 - Rom)

JERRY HARDIN
(Magistrate Radue - TNG: WHEN THE BOUGH BREAKS)

(Samuel Clemens - TNG: TIME'S ARROW I-11)

ROBERT O'REILLY
(Holodeck Thug - TNG: MANHUNT)

(Gawron - TNG: THE REUNION/ REDEMPTION I-II/ RIGHTFUL HEIR)

SUZIE PLAKSON
(Dr. Selar - TNG: THE SCHIZOID MAN)

(K'Ehleyr - TNG: THE EMISSARY/ THE REUNION)

JOHN PUTCH
(Benzite Cadet Mordok - TNG: COMING OF AGE)

(Benzite Ensign Mendon - TNG: A MATTER OF HONOR)

CAROLYN SEYMOUR
(Romulan Subcommander Toras - TNG: CONTAGION)

(Mirastra Yale - TNG: FIRST CONTACT)

(Romulan Commander Torel - TNG: FACE OF THE ENEMY)

LANCE SPELLERBERG
(Transporter Chief - TNG: WE'LL ALWAYS HAVE PARIS)

(Ensign Herbert - TNG: THE ICARUS FACTOR)

Lavar Burton at the 1994 NAACP awards.   Photo c 1994 Albert L. Ortega

A Next Generation Celebration   **147**

PATRICK STEWART
(TNG - Captain Jean-Luc Picard)
(Locutus of Borg - TNG: BEST OF
BOTH WORLDS I-II)

BRAD ZERBST
(Medical Officer - TNG: JUSTICE)
(Nurse - TNG: HEART OF GLORY/
SKIN OF EVIL)

MULTIPLE TNG APPEARANCES AS SAME CHARACTER

RHONDA ALDRICH
(Holodeck Secretary Madelyn - TNG:
THE BIG GOODBYE/ MANHUNT/
CLUES)

JONATHAN DEL ARCO
(Hugh of Borg - TNG: I, BORG,
DESCENT II)

BRIAN BONSALL
(Alexander Rozhenko - TNG: NEW
GROUND/ COST OF LIVING/
ETHICS/ IMAGINARY FRIEND/ RAS-
CALS/ A FISTFUL OF DATAS)
(Alexander was played by JON STEUER
in TNG: THE REUNION)

GEORGIA BROWN
(Helena Rozhenko - TNG - FAMILY/
NEW GROUND)

WARD COSTELLO
(Admiral Gregory Quinn - TNG: COM-
ING OF AGE/ CONSPIRACY)

DENISE CROSBY
(Sela - TNG: THE MIND'S
EYES/REDEMPTION I-II/ UNIFICA-
TION I-II)
(Security Chief Tasha Yar/ episodes 1-22)
(Alternate Tasha Yar - TNG: YESTER-
DAY'S ENTERPRISE)

CHARLES COOPER
(K'mpec - TNG: SINS OF THE
FATHER/ THE REUNION)

DANIEL DAVIS
(Professor James Moriarty - TNG: ELE-
MENTARY, DEAR DATA/ SHIP IN A
BOTTLE)

SHEILA FRANKLIN
(Ensign - NEW GROUND/ HERO
WORSHIP/ THE MASTERPIECE SOCI-
ETY/ A MATTER OF TIME/ IMAGI-
NARY FRIEND)

SUSAN GIBNEY
(Dr. Leah Brahms - TNG: BOOBY
TRAP/ GALAXY'S CHILD)

JOHN HANCOCK
(Admiral Haden - TNG: THE DEFEC-
TOR/ THE WOUNDED)

JENNIFER HETRICK
(Vash - TNG: CAPTAIN'S HOLIDAY/
Q-PID)
(Vash - DS9: Q-LESS)

ASHLEY JUDD
(Mission Specialist Robin Leffler - TNG:
DARMOK/ THE GAME)

ANDREAS KATSULAS
(Romulan Commander Tomalak - TNG:
THE ENEMY/ THE DEFECTOR/
FUTURE IMPERFECT)

CLYDE KUSATSU
(Admiral Nakamura - TNG: THE MEA-
SURE OF A MAN/ PHANTASMS)

PATRICK MASSETT
(Duras - TNG: SINS OF THE FATHER/
THE REUNION)

CAROLYN McCORMICK
(Minuet - TNG: 11001001/ FUTURE
IMPERFECT)

ERIC MENYUK
(The Traveler - TNG: WHERE NO ONE
HAS GONE BEFORE/ REMEMBER ME)

JOANNA MILES
(Perrin - TNG: SAREK/ UNIFICATION
I)

LYCIA NAFF
(Ensign Sonya Gomez - TNG: Q WHO?/
SAMARITAN SNARE)

NATALIJA NOGULICH
(Admiral N'Chiev - TNG: CHAIN OF
COMMAND I-II/ DESCENT I)

ROBERT O'REILLY
(Holodeck Thug - TNG: MANHUNT)
(Gawron - TNG: THE REUNION/
REDEMPTION I-II/ RIGHTFUL HEIR)

SUZIE PLAKSON
(K'EHLYER - TNG: THE EMISSARY/
THE REUNION)
(Dr. Selar - TNG: THE SCHIZOID
MAN)

MICHAEL RIDER
(Transporter Chief - TNG: THE NAKED
NOW/ CODE OF HONOR/ HAVEN)

ROBERT SCHENKKAN
(Commander Dexter Remmick - TNG:
COMING OF AGE/ CONSPIRACY)

DWIGHT SCHULTZ
(Lt. Reginald "Reg" Barclay - TNG:
HOLLOW PURSUITS/ THE NTH
DEGREE/ REALM OF FEAR/ SHIP IN A
BOTTLE/ GENESIS)

CAREL STRUYCKEN
(Mr. Homm - TNG: HAVEN/ MAN-
HUNT/ MENAGE A TROI/ HALF A
LIFE/ COST OF LIVING)

KEN THORLEY
(Bolian Barber Mr. Mott - TNG:
ENSIGN RO/ SCHISMS)

TONY TODD
(Klingon Commander Kurn - TNG: SINS
OF THE FATHER/ REDEMPTION I-II)

Michael Dorn at the 1993 Las Vegas Paramount Booth for the VSDA convention.

JULIE WARNER
(Christy Henshaw - TNG: BOOBY
TRAP/ TRANSFIGURATIONS)

DOUG WERT
(Jack Crusher - TNG: FAMILY/ VIOLA-
TIONS)

PATTI YASUTAKE
(Nurse Marissa Ogawa - ETHICS/
IMAGINARY FRIEND/ CAUSE AND
EFFECT/ THE INNER LIGHT/ THE
GAME/ CLUES/ SUSPICIONS)
(Alternate Dr. Ogawa - TNG: PARAL-
LELS)

BIFF YEAGER
(Asst. Chief Engineer Argyle - TNG:
DATALORE/ WHERE NO ONE HAS
GONE BEFORE)

MULTIPLE TNG AND DS9 APPEARANCES AS DIFFERENT CHARACTERS

MARC ALAIMO
(Antican Delegate - TNG: LONELY
AMONG US)
(DS9: Companion)
(Romulan Commander T'Bok - TNG:
THE NEUTRAL ZONE)
(Cardassian Gul Macet - TNG: THE
WOUNDED)
(1880's Gambler - TNG: TIME'S
ARROW I)

(Gul Dukat - DS9 - EMISSARY I-II/
DUET/ THE HOMECOMING/ CAR-
DASSIANS)

MICHAEL ENSIGN
(Krola - TNG: FIRST CONTACT)
(DS9: IF WISHES WERE HORSES)

MAX GRODENCHIK
(DS9 - Rom)
(Sovak - TNG: CAPTAIN'S HOLIDAY)
(Par Lenor - TNG: THE PERFECT
MATE)

ANNE HANEY
(Bajoran Arbiter - DS9: DAX)
(Rishan Uxbridge - TNG: THE SUR-
VIVORS)

MICHAEL HORAN
(Lt. Barnaby - TNG: DESCENT II)
(Alien Captain - DS9: CAPTIVE PUR-
SUIT)

ARMIN SHIMERMAN
(DS9 - Quark)
(Talking Wedding Box - TNG: HAVEN)
(Ledek - TNG: THE LAST OUTPOST)
(Bractor - TNG: PEAK PERFOR-
MANCE)

MULTIPLE TNG AND DS9 APPEARANCES AS SAME CHARACTER

MAJEL BARRETT
(Lwaxana Troi - DS9: THE FORSAKEN)
(Lwaxana Troi - TNG: HAVEN/ MAN-HUNT/ MENAGE A TROI/ HALF A LIFE/ COST OF LIVING)
(Number One - CT: THE CAGE)
(Nurse/Dr. Christine Chapel - (see CT) plus ST:TMP/ST IV: TVH/ ST VI: TUC)

JOHN de LANCIE
(Q - DS9: Q-LESS)
(Q - TNG: ENCOUNTER AT FAR-POINT I-II/ HIDE AND Q/ Q WHO?/ DEJA Q/ Q-PID/ TRUE Q/ TAPESTRY)

SIDDIG EL FADIL
(DS9 - Dr. Julian Bashir)
(Dr. Bashir - TNG: BIRTHRIGHT I)

HANA HATAE
(Molly Worf Ishikawa O'Brien - TNG: RASCALS)
(Molly - DS9: A MAN ALONE/ IF WISHES WERE HORSES/ IN THE HANDS OF THE PROPHETS/ THE SIEGE)

JENNIFER HETRICK
(Vash - DS9: Q-LESS)
(Vash - TNG: CAPTAIN'S HOLIDAY/ Q-PID)

BARBARA MARCH
(Lursa - TNG: REDEMPTION I-II)
(Lursa - DS9: PAST PROLOGUE)

MULTIPLE TNG AND STAR TREK FILM CHARACTERS

MAJEL BARRETT (see other listings)

MERRITT BUTRICK
(Dr. David Marcus - ST II: THE WRATH OF KHAN/ ST III: TSFS)
(Captain Tejun - TNG: SYMBIOSIS)

ROBIN CURTIS
(Saavik - ST III: THE SEARCH FOR SPOCK/ ST IV: THE VOYAGE HOME)
(T'Lera/T'Paul - TNG: GAMBIT I-II)

MICHAEL DORN
(TNG - Lt. Worf)
(Colonel Worf - ST VI: TUC)

ROBERT ELLENSTEIN
(Federation President Axelrod - ST IV: TVH)
(Stephen Miller - TNG: HAVEN)

MARK LENARD (see other listings)

GEORGE MURDOCK
(Admiral J.P. Hanson - TNG: BEST OF BOTH WORLDS I-II)
(Godlike Alien Entity - ST V: THE FINAL FRONTIER)

Michael Dorn   Photo c 1994 Albert L. Ortega

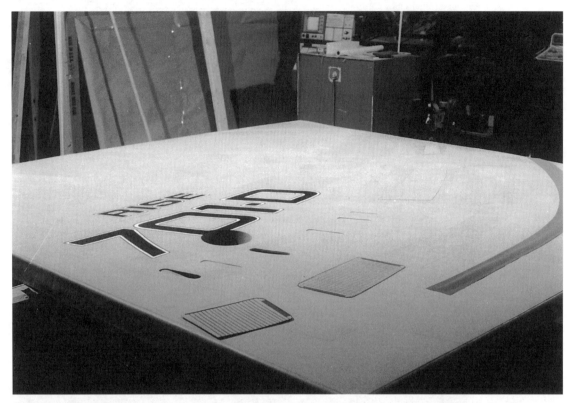

Scorches being prepared on the surface of the Enterprise for the *Q-Who* episode.
Photo c 1994 "Deep Focus"

JUDSON SCOTT
(Joaquim - ST II: TWOK)
(Sobi - TNG: SYMBIOSIS)

MADGE SINCLAIR
(Saratoga Captain - ST IV: TVH)
(Captain LaForge - TNG: INTERFACE)

DAVID WARNER
(Terran Ambassador St. John Talbot - ST V: TFF)
(Klingon Chancellor Gorkon - ST VI: THE UNDISCOVERED COUNTRY)
(Cardassian Gul Madred - TNG: CHAIN OF COMMAND I-II)

MULTIPLE TNG/CT/STAR TREK FILM APPEARANCES AS SAME CHARACTER

JAMES DOOHAN
(CT - Chief Engineer Commander Montgomery Scott)
(Captain Montgomery Scott - TNG: RELICS)

DeFOREST KELLEY
(CT - Chief Medical Officer Dr. Leonard "Bones" McCoy)
(Admiral Leonard McCoy - TNG: ENCOUNTER AT FARPOINT)

MARK LENARD
(Ambassador Sarek - CT: JOURNEY TO

BABEL/ ST III: TSFS/ ST IV: TVH/ ST V: TFF/ ST VI: TUC) (TNG: SAREK/ UNIFICATION I)
(Romulan Commander - CT: BALANCE OF TERROR)
(Klingon Captain - ST: TMP)

RICARDO MONTALBAN
(Khan Noonian Singh - CT: SPACE SEED/ ST II: TWOK)

LEONARD NIMOY
(CT - Mr. Spock)
(Ambassador Spock - TNG: UNIFICATION I-II)

JANE WYATT
(Amanda Grayson - CT: JOURNEY TO BABEL/ ST IV: TVH)

MULTIPLE TNG AND CT APPEARANCES AS DIFFERENT CHARACTERS

MAJEL BARRETT
(Lwaxana Troi - DS9: THE FORSAKEN)
(TNG: HAVEN/MANHUNT/ MENAGE A TROI/ HALF A LIFE/ COST OF LIVING)
(Number One - CT: THE CAGE)
(Nurse/Dr. Christine Chapel - CT: ST: TMP/ ST IV: TVH/ ST VI: TUC)

MERRITT BUTRICK
(Dr. David Marcus - ST II: TWOK/ ST III: TSFS)
(Captain Tejun - TNG: SYMBIOSIS)

MARK LENARD
(Ambassador Sarek - CT: JOURNEY TO BABEL/ ST III: TSFS/ST IV: TVH. ST V: TFF/ ST VI: TUC) (TNG: SAREK/ UNIFICATION I)
(Romulan Commander - CT: BALANCE OF TERROR)
(Klingon Captain - ST: THE MOTION PICTURE)

PHIL MORRIS
(Ensign - ST III: TSFS)
(Gang Member - TNG: LEGACY)

DIANA MULDAUR
(TNG - Dr. Katherine Pulaski)
(Dr. Anne Mulhall/Thalessa - CT: RETURN TO TOMORROW)
(Dr. Miranda Jones - CT: IS THERE IN TRUTH NO BEAUTY?)

JUDSON SCOTT
(Joaquim - ST II: TWOK)
(Sobi - TNG: SYMBIOSIS)

MALACHI THRONE
(Commodore Jose Mendez - CT: THE MENAGERIE)
(Romulan Senator Pardek - TNG: UNIFICATION I-II)
(Voice - Talosian Keeper - CT: THE CAGE)

PAUL WINFIELD
(Captain Terrell - ST II: TWOK)
(Tamarian Captain Dathon - TNG: DARMOK)

TNG GUEST STARS

MADCHEN AMICK
(Anya as Teenage Girl - TNG: THE DAUPHIN)

ERICH ANDERSON
(Commander MacDuff - TNG: CONUNDRUM)

FRAN BENNETT
(Admiral - TNG: REDEMPTION II)

THEODORE BIKEL
(Sergei Rozhenko - TNG: FAMILY)

ROBIN CURTIS
(T'Lera/T'Paul - TNG: GAMBIT I-II)
(Saavik - ST III: TSFS/ ST IV: TVH)

SUSAN DIOL
(Carmen - TNG: SILICON AVATAR)

JAMES DOOHAN
(Captain Montgomery Scott - TNG: RELICS)

SAMANTHA EGGAR
(Marie Picard - TNG: FAMILY)

MICK FLEETWOOD
(Antedian Assassin - TNG: MANHUNT)

MATT FREWER
(Professor Berlingoff Rasmussen - TNG: A MATTER OF TIME)

ELLEN GEER
(Dr. Marr - TNG: THE SILICON AVATAR)

WALTER GOTELL
(Director Kurt Mandel - TNG: HOME SOIL)

KELSEY GRAMMER
(Captain Morgan Bateman - TNG: CAUSE AND EFFECT)

TERRY HATCHER
(Lt. Wells - TNG: THE OUTRAGEOUS OKONA)

DR. STEPHEN W. HAWKING
(Holodeck Stephen Hawking - TNG: DESCENT I)

ROBERT ITO
(Tech Officer Chang - TNG: COMING OF AGE)

FAMKE JANSSEN
(Kamala - TNG: THE PERFECT MATE)

ASHLEY JUDD
(Mission Specialist Robin Leffler - TNG: DARMOK/ THE GAME)

DeFOREST KELLEY
(Admiral Leonard "Bones" McCoy - TNG: ENCOUNTER AT FARPOINT)

JEREMY KEMP
(Robert Picard - TNG: FAMILY)

NORMAN LARGE
(Romulan Proconsul Neral - TNG: UNI-
FICATION I-II)

ED LAUTER
(Lt. Commander Albert - TNG: THE
FIRST DUTY)

NORMAN LLOYD
(Professor Galen - TNG: THE CHASE)

MARK AND BRIAN
(Evolved crewmen - TNG: IDENTITY
CRISIS)

KATHERINE MOFFAT
(Etana - TNG: THE GAME)

BEBE NEUWIRTH
(Lanel - TNG: FIRST CONTACT)

JULIA NICKSON
(Lee Ann Su - TNG: THE ARSENAL OF
FREEDOM)

LEONARD NIMOY
(Ambassador Spock - TNG: UNIFICA-
TION I-II)

TIM O'CONNOR
(Krios Ambassador Briam - TNG: THE
PERFECT MATE)

MICHELLE PHILLIPS
(Jenice Manheim - TNG: WE'LL
ALWAYS HAVE PARIS)

JOE PISCOPO
(Holodeck Comedian - TNG: THE
OUTRAGEOUS OKONA)

CLIFF POTTS
(Admiral Kennelly - TNG: ENSIGN RO)

JEAN SIMMONS
(Admiral Sartie - TNG: THE DRUM-
HEAD)

PAUL SORVINO
(Michael Rozhenko - TNG: HOME-
WARD)

JOHN TESH
(Klingon - TNG: THE ICARUS FAC-
TOR)

KEN THORLEY
(Bolian Barber Mr. Mott - TNG:
ENSIGN RO/ SCHISMS)

MALACHI THRONE
(Romulan Senator Pardek - TNG: UNI-
FICATION I-II)
(Commodore Jose Mendez - CT: THE
MENAGERIE)
(Voice - Talosian Keeper - CT: THE
CAGE)

BEN VEREEN
(Dr. LaForge - TNG: INTERFACE)

RAY WALSTON
(Boothby - TNG: THE FIRST DUTY)

RAY WISE
(Liko - TNG: WHO WATCHES THE
WATCHERS)

JAMES WORTHY
(Korath - TNG: GAMBIT II)

THE SECRET LIFE OF THE ENTERPRISE

How technical is the futuristic technology worked out for the Enterprise? It's more complicated than you think as the "technobabble" (as the actors call their dialogue) all actually means something as the following piece about the inner workings of the Enterprise aptly demonstrates. This piece is not for those who are technologically faint at heart…

It's the real star of THE NEXT GENERATION—a sleek spacefaring craft, the most advanced of its kind, carrying over a thousand people on a mission of exploration. As much a city as a ship, the Enterprise-D is the pride of Starfleet.

Here's a look at the secret life of this star, without which Jean-Luc Picard and crew would be dismally and boringly earthbound.

The Enterprise is categorized as an Explorer, the largest starship in a fleet that includes Cruisers, Cargo Carriers, Tankers, Surveyors, and Scout ships. Able to carry out deep space exploration, including full biologic and ecological studies, charting and mapping, first contact scenarios as well as ambassadorial missions. The Enterprise is also equipped for defense, though this is not its primary mission parameter.

Sensor capabilities include gravimetric, optical, quark population analysis, subspace flux, particle, and full spectrum EM. The Enterprise is capable of wide-band life sciences analysis. It has the ability to support both on-board and probe-mounted science instrumentation. Instrumentation includes multimode neutrino interferometry and two-meter diameter gamma ray telescope.

The Enterprise is able to support a wide number of mission-related ongoing research and other projects. Sufficient habitable volume and power generation for facilities exist. There is no undue impact on primary mission operations. Two independent launch, supply, and repair bays are provided as support facilities for auxiliary spacecraft and instrumented probes.

CREW ENVIRONMENT

The life support of the Enterprise is designed to sustain Class M (Earth style) compatible oxygen-breathing personnel. Systems are triply redundant. The Enterprise can be adapted to Class H, Class L, Or Class K environmental conditions.

Facilities to support Class M compatible personnel are present in all living quarters. Ten percent of quarters are able to support Class H, K, and L conditions. An additional two percent of quarters are equipped for Class N and N(2) environmental conditions.

Habitable area includes 800,000 m2 for mission-adaptable facilities, including living quarters. These areas are to be protected from Em and nuclear radiation by an SFRA-standard 347.3(a) level. Subspace flux differential is kept within 0.02 millicochranes.

TACTICAL

Defense systems include a full array of Type X phaser bank elements for both primary and battle sections capable of 5.1MW maximum single emitter output. One photon torpedo launcher is required for the primary hull, and two are required for the battle section.

The Enterprise D is able to separate into two separate spacecraft: A battle section capable of warp flight and optimized for combat, and a primary section capable of impulse flight and defensive operations. The command section has full autonomous sublight operational capacity.

The defensive shielding systems of the ship exceed 7.3 x 105kW primary energy dissipation rate. These systems are fully redundant, with the auxiliary system able to provide 65% of the protection of the primary system.

THE HISTORY OF THE ENTERPRISE-D

The Enterprise D has a useful life of approximately one hundred years. An estimated five major ship-wide system swapouts and upgrades are performed on the Enterprise at regular intervals of twenty years or so. Minor upgrades and repairs are scheduled every one to five years.

Few other ships in Starfleet have been so recognized as the original Enterprise. The Enterprise D is the fourth successor to the name and number of the first Enterprise, NCC-1701.

The first Enterprise was a Constitution class starship. Captain April, Captain Christopher Pike, and Captain James T. Kirk piloted the ship in succession. Under James Kirk the Enterprise became a historic figure in deep space exploration. It was destroyed in 2285 while defending the Mutara sector against a Klingon attack.

The second Enterprise NCC-1701-A in 2286 was originally christened the Yorktown. It was also a Constitution class ship. The ship was renamed Enterprise and assigned to Captain Kirk following his role, and that of his crew, in defending the planet Earth from an alien space-craft. This ship also aided in the success of the Khitomer conference.

The third Enterprise, NCC-1701-B was an Excelsior class ship. This ship and her crew explored space beyond the Gourami quadrant, mapping over 142 star systems and contacting seventeen civilizations.

The fourth Enterprise, NCC-1701-C was an Ambassador class ship commanded by Captain Rachel Garrett. This ship was lost in 2344 near the Narendra system attempting to defend a Klingon outpost from Romulan attackers. This bravery led to the current alliance between the Federation and the Klingon Empire.

The fifth Enterprise, NCC-1701-D, is Galaxy class starship commissioned in 2363. This starship is under the command of Captain Jean-Luc Picard. This latest starship has already distinguished itself with many heroic efforts defending the security of the Federation, as well as a number of significant missions of exploration.

THE STRUCTURE OF THE FICTIONAL ENTERPRISE

The exterior hulls are reinforced against flight stresses by energy fields that actively compensate for internal and external forces. Structures built into the hulls allow for a variety of functions.

The bridge provides command of phaser arrays, photon torpedo launchers and subspace radio arrays. Windows give crewmembers needed vistas.

The forty-two decks are divided around major load-bearing structures. Many systems are suspended within the open spaces, "floating" on flexible ligaments that minimize mechanical, thermal, and conductive shocks. At the launch of the Enterprise, 35% of the internal volume was not yet filled with room modules. This empty spaceframe remains open for future expansion and mission applications.

The living areas of the starship have been designed with the comfort and the safety of the crew in mind during their long periods of flight. 110 square meters of living space are provided per person, in addition to shared space and areas devoted for purely working functions.

STRUCTURAL SPECIFICATIONS

The main frame of the Enterprise is fabricated from an interlocking series of tritanium/duranium macrofilament truss frames. They average 1.27 m2 in cross section. Many of these trusses are integral to the main and saucer impulse engine regions, both saucer and battle sides of the docking latch interfaces, the warp nacelle pylons, and along the centerlines of the hull structure. Smaller trusses provide supports within the deck and core structure of the interior of the spacecraft.

Parallel aluminum crystalfoam stringers are bonded to the primary trusses to provide low frequency vibration attenuation across the main structure. These stringers also support certain utility conduits. Various conformed devices are attached to the stringers and built into the hull structure. These include subspace radio antennas, and elements of the deflector shield grid, which are incorporated into the exterior skin of the Enterprise.

A secondary framework of microextruded terminium trusses are mounted to the primary spaceframe and attached to the inner hull structure. The secondary framework is mounted by support rods to allow some freedom from the primary frame, allowing relief of mechanical strain and some vibration and noise isolation. The secondary framework segments are also separated from each other to allow replacement and repair of infrastructure.

A series of forcefields provide structural integrity to the Enterprise in flight. The force field energy is distributed through a network of waveguides, which in turn distribute the energy into ceramic-polymer conductive elements throughout the frame. Without the reinforcement of the forcefields, the Enterprise would sag under its own weight in Earth's gravity.

The primary load-bearing trusses join the exterior hull substrate through electron bonded duranium pins at 1.25 meter intervals. These pins are fitted into an insulating ceramic fabric jacket that provides thermal insulation between the exterior hull and the frame. These elements are gamma-welded together.

THE STRUCTURAL INTEGRITY FIELD SYSTEM

The integrity of the spaceframe is augmented by the Structural Integrity Field System. It is a network of force field segments that compensate for structural load factors that would otherwise exceed the mechanical limits of the spaceframe.

Field generation is provided by three field generators placed on Deck 11 in the Primary Hull and also by two generators on Deck 32 of the Secondary Hull. Each generator is a cluster of twenty MW graviton polarity sources leading into a pair of 250 millicochrane subspace field distortion amplifiers. Thermal dissipation is provided by continuous-action liquid helium coolant loops. Two backup generators exist in each hull, able to provide up to twelve hours of use at 55% of maximum power.

Operating rules during cruise mode demand at least one generator to be active in each hull. Activation of a second generator is allowed during extreme maneuvers. In case of reduced power, a single field generator can feed the entire frame by using a field conduit connection between the primary and engineering sections.

INERTIA DAMPING SYSTEM

This system generates a controlled series of variable-symmetry forcefields

The Enterprise's engine room.
Photo c 1994 "Deep Focus"

which operate to absorb inertial forces of space flight that would harm the living crew inside. The forcefields for the inertia damping system are generated independently from the Structural Integrity Field. The IDF is fed by a parallel series of waveguides to the synthetic gravity plates.

A low level force field is maintained throughout the habitable sections of the Enterprise. As acceleration effects are anticipated, this field is distorted along a vector opposite to the velocity change. The

IDF is subject to a lag time in shifting direction and intensity. Because control of the inertia damping system is normally derived from Flight Controller data, normal course corrections are anticipated, and detectable effects of acceleration are avoided. If power for IDF operations becomes limited or sudden maneuvers or externally caused accelerations occur, the lag time becomes noticeable.

Normally at least two field generators are active at all times in each hull. Additional units can be

brought on-line during anticipation of extreme maneuvers. During an alert, all units are brought to standby for immediate activation. If the Enterprise is operating under reduced power, a single field generator is capable of feeding the entire spaceframe, using the field conduit connections between the primary and engineering sections.

WARP AND IMPULSE DRIVE

While warp field theory is within the accepted limits of general physics in the STAR TREK universe, it circumvents the limits of General, Special and Transformational Relativity. Early warp engines managed superluminal flight by straddling the speed of light, alternating at two velocity states while remaining at neither for no longer than Planck time, 1.3 x 10 to the -43rd second, the smallest possible unit of measured time. This has the net effect of maintaining velocities at the speed of light, while avoiding theoretically infinite energy expenditures that would otherwise be required.

Later CDP (informally dubbed 'warp' engines) would eventually avoid straddling the speed of light altogether by exploring the realm of subspace that lay on the other side.

The key to the creation of propulsion not dependent on exhaustive reaction products depends on the concept of layering many fields of warp energy, each layer exerting a controlled amount of force against the outermost neighbor. The combined effect of the force applied drives the ship forward. This combined force is known as asymmetrical peristatic field, manipulatorion, or APFM. Warp field coils in the energy nacelles are energized in sequence, fore to aft. The firing frequency then determines the number of field layers-the greater the number of layers per unit time, the higher the warp speed. Each new field layer expands outward from the nacelle, experiences a rapid force coupling and decoupling at variable distances from the nacelles, at the same time transferring energy and separating from the previous layer at speeds between o.5C and o.9C.

During force coupling the radiated energy makes the transition into subspace, applying a visible mass reduction effect to the spacecraft. This allows the spacecraft to slip through the sequential layers of warp field energy.

INSIDE WARP

The Cochrane is the energy unit used to measure subspace field stress. Generated fields below Warp factor one are measured in millicochranes. It is a tribute to Zefram Cochrane, who along with his engineering team, devised the basic mechanism of continuum distortion propulsion-CDC, or warp drive. Cochranes are also used to measure field distortion created by other spatial manipulation devices like tractor beams, deflectors, and synthetic gravity fields.

A subspace field of one thousand millocochranes or greater creates the effect of the normal warp field. Field intensity for each warp factor increases geometrically and is a function of the total of the individual field value layers. The cochrane value for a given warp factor corresponds to the apparent velocity of a spacecraft traveling at that warp factor. As an example, a ship traveling at warp factor 4 is maintaining a warp field of at least 102 cochranes. therefore traveling at 102 times the speed of light. At Warp 10, the field intensity is infinite and cannot be reached.

Warp fields that exceed a given warp factor but do not cross the threshold to the next higher level are called fractional warp factors. Travel at a given warp factor can be markedly faster than travel at the next lower warp factor, but for extended space travel, it is often more energy efficient to simply raise the energy level to the next higher warp factor.

The actual values are dependent on interstellar conditions. Gas density, electric and magnetic fields and fluctuations in the subspace domain affect the efficacy of warp drive. Starships travel at multiple warp factors as a matter of routine, but they suffer from energy penalties as a result of the quantum drag forces and motive power oscillation inefficiencies.

The energy required to initiate the warp field is greater than the energy required to maintain it. Called the peak transitional threshold, once it has been crossed, the amount of power required to maintain a given warp field is lessened. While the Enterprise engine designs allow for control of unprecedented amounts of energy, the efficacy of the warp driver coil electrodynamic decreases as warp field increases.

MEASURING WARP FACTORS

Warp Factors
Factor 1 = 1 cochrane
Factor 2 = 10 cochranes
Factor 3 = 39 cochranes
Factor 4 = 102 cochranes
Factor 5 = 214 cochranes
Factor 6 = 392 cochranes
Factor 7 = 656 cochranes
Factor 8 = 1024 cochranes
Factor 9 = 1516 cochranes

The warp propulsion system of the Enterprise consists of three assemblies: the matter/antimatter reaction assembly, power transfer conduits, and warp engine nacelles. While propelling the Enterprise through space, this system also powers such essential systems as the defense shields, phaser arrays, tractor beam, main deflector, and computer cores.

The matter/antimatter reaction assembly, M/ARA is the heart of the warp propulsion system. The M/ARA is superior to other methods of power generation because of the 10 to the 6th power times greater energy output of the matter-antimatter reaction over that of standard fusion, as is used in the impulse propulsion system. It is variously called the warp reactor, warp engine core, or the main engine core. Energy produced within the assembly is divided between the propulsion of the Enterprise and servicing the major ship systems.

The warp reactor is made up of four subsys-

tems: the magnetic constriction segments, the power transfer conduits, the matter/antimatter reaction chamber, and the reactant injectors.

MATTER/ANTI-MATTER

The reactant injectors manufacture and feed precisely controlled streams of matter and antimatter into the core. The matter reactant injector, the MRI, accepts supercold deuterium from the primary deuterium tankage, the PDT, in the upper bulge of the Engineering hull and partially preburns it in a continuous gas-fusion process. It then drives the gases through a series of throttleable nozzles into the upper magnetic constriction segment. The MRI is a conical structural vessel. Twenty-five shock attenuation cylinders connect it to the PDI and the major spacecraft framing members on Deck 30, achieving 98% thermal insulation from the remainder of the Battle Section. In effect, the WPS 'floats' within the engineering hull in order to withstand the operational stresses.

Within the matter reactant injector are six redundant cross-fed sets of injectors. Each injector includes twin deuterium inlet manifold fuel conditioners, magnetic quench blocks, transfer duct/gas combiner, fusion preburner, nozzle head, and related control hardware. Slush deuterium enters the inlet manifolds at controlled

Close-up of "core sample" from the episode _Q Who_.   Photo c 1994 "Deep Focus"

rates and passes to the manifold fuel conditioners, where thermal energy is removed to bring the slush deuterium slightly above the solid transition point. Micropellets form within the slush, are preburned by the magnetic pinch fusion, and are sent down into the gas combiner, where the ionized gas products reach a level of 10 to the 6th power K. The nozzle heads then focus, align, and direct the gas streams into the constriction segments.

Opposite of the matter reactant injector is the antimatter injector. The design and operation of the antimatter injector is markedly different than that of the MRI due to the hazards of dealing with antimatter fuel. Steps in manipulating and injecting antihydrogen are protected by magnetic fields to isolate the fuel from the spacecraft structure and stresses. The ARI requires fewer moving components than the MRI, employing the same basic structural housing and shock attenuation struts, with adaptations for magnetic-suspension fuel tunnels.

THE REACTION CHAMBER

The magnetic constriction segments structurally support the matter/antimatter reaction chamber and provide a pressure vessel to maintain the proper core operating environment. They align the incoming matter and antimatter reaction chambers.

A typical magnetic constriction segment carries eight sets of tension frame members, a toroidal pressure vessel wall, twelve sets of magnetic constrictor coils, and related power feed and control hardware. The outermost transparent layer of the segments allows for a visible gauge of engine performance, as weak secondary photons are emitted from the inner layers. This creates the characteristic blue glow visible in the chamber.

The matter/antimatter reaction chamber is comprised of two matched bell-shaped cavities which contain and redirect the initial reaction. Situated on the equator of the chamber is the dilithium crystal articulation frame, the DCAF. The DCAF consists of an EM-isolated cradle designed to hold approximately 1200 cm3 of dilithium crystal, and two redundant sets of three-axis crystal orientation linkages. The crystal must be directed within six degrees of freedom to achieve the proper angles and depths or reaction mediation.

Dilithium crystal is the only material known to Federation science to be nonreactive with antimatter when subjected to a high-frequency electromagnetic field in the megawatt range. The dilithium crystals become receptive to antihydrogen, permitting it to pass directly through the crystalline structure without actually coming in contact with it because of the field dynamo effect generated in the added iron atoms.

POWER TRANSFER CONDUITS

The power transfer conduits are similar to the constrictor segments as they constrain plasma to the center of twin channels and peristaltically force the plasma toward the warp engine nacelles, where the warp field coils utilize the energy for propulsion. The power transfer conduits extend from Engineering aft, where they intercept the warp engine support pylons.

The termination point for the energetic plasma passed along the power transfer conduits is the warp field nacelles. This is where the actual propulsion takes place. Each nacelle includes the warp field coils, a plasma injection system, a maintenance docking port and an emergency separation system.'

The plasma injection system sits at the end of the power transfer conduits. The system is comprised of a series of magnetic injectors linked to the warp-engine controllers. The warp field coils generate an intense, multilayered field that surrounds the Enterprise, aided by the ship's structural design. It is the manipulation of the shape of this field that allows propulsion beyond the speed of light. The maintenance docking port allows any work pod of shuttle pod to attach, permitting engineering crews and hardware.

FUELING THE WARP DRIVE

Deuterium tankers are responsible for refueling the Enterprise while in space. Two deuterium loading ports are located along the structural spine of the Battle section, aft of the "tail" of the deuterium tank.

In the event the Enterprise cannot rendezvous with a tanker, it has the capability of pulling low grade matter from the interstellar medium through a series of high-energy coils known collectively as a Bussard ramscoop. The concept of using electromagnetic fields to collect hydrogen for fuel use in space was proposed by physicist Dr. Robert W. Bussard in the 1960's.

The Enterprise is also capable of generating small amounts of antimatter during emergency situations. As it is both power and matter intensive, using the antimatter generator is also an emergency measure.

IMPULSE DRIVE

Sublight propulsion of the Enterprise and some auxiliary functions of the ship are handled by the impulse propulsion system. Two sets of fusion-powered engines comprise the IPS: the main impulse engine, comprised of four individual impulse engines, and the Saucer Module impulse engines, comprised of two groups of engines.

During normal operation the main impulse engine is used to provide thrust for interplanetary and sublight interstellar flight. High impulse operations may require the added use of the Saucer Module impulse engines. These operations are avoided as much as duly possible due to the inherent time distortion and relativistic considerations.

The fuel supplies for the impulse drive are contained within the primary deuterium tank in the Battle Section and in a set of thirty-two auxiliary cryo tanks in the Saucer Module. While the primary deuterium tank is normally loaded with slush deuterium, the cryo reactants in the Saucer Module are liquid. In the event that fuel supplies must be acquired from the main tank, thermal energy is added to the slush deuterium to allow proper fuel flow. In emergency situations, minute amounts of antimatter may be injected into the impulse reaction chamber in the event that short periods of overthrust or increased power generation are required. There is no way to transfer antimatter between the Saucer

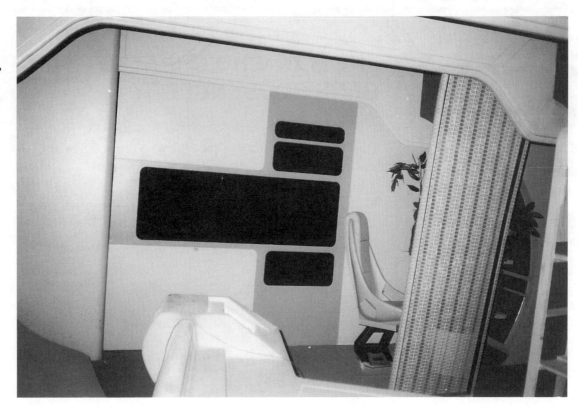

module tanks and the primary tank in the Battle Section.

The main impulse engine is located on Deck 23 of the Enterprise. It runs along the centerline of the docked spacecraft. If the Saucer Module is separated from the Battle section, then the engine thrust bectors are adjusted to point up slightly from the center to adjust for the new center of balance.

HOW THE IMPULSE ENGINES WORK

Each individual impulse engine consists of three basic components. The impulse engine consists of three basic components. Three impulse reaction chambers are allocated per impulse engine. This IRC is an armored sphere designed to contain the energy released in a conventional proton-proton fusion reaction. The Enterprise normally carries four

additional IRC modules as backup power generation devices, though the modules may be used to provide backup propulsion. An accelerator/generator, a driver coil assembly, and a vectored exhaust director completes the assembly.

THE MAN WHO CREATED STAR TREK: GENE RODDENBERRY

James Van Hise

The complete life story of the man who created STAR TREK, reveals the man and his work.

$14.95 in stores ONLY $12.95 to Couch Potato Catalog Customers
160 Pages
ISBN # 1-55698-318-2

TWENTY-FIFTH ANNIVERSARY TREK TRIBUTE

James Van Hise

Taking a close up look at the amazing Star Trek stroy, this book traces the history of the show that has become an enduring legend. James Van Hise chronicles the series from 1966 to its cancellation in 1969, through the years when only the fans kept it alive, and on to its unprecedented revival. He offers a look at its latter-day blossoming into an animated series, a sequence of five movies (with a sixth in preparation) that has grossed over $700 million, and the offshoot "The Next Generation" TV series.

The author gives readers a tour of the memorials at the Smithsonian and the Movieland Wax Museums, lets them witness Leonard Nimoy get his star on the Hollywood Walk Of Fame in 1985, and takes them behind the scenes of the motion-picture series and TV's "The Next Generation." The concluding section examines the future of Star Trek beyond its 25th Anniversary.

$14.95.....196 Pages
ISBN # 1-55698-290-9

COUCH POTATO INC. 5715 N. Balsam Rd Las Vegas, NV 89130 (702)658-2090

Use Your Credit Card 24 HRS — Order toll Free From: **(800)444-2524** Ext 67

THE HISTORY OF TREK

James Van Hise

The complete story of Star Trek from Original conception to its effects on millions of Lives across the world. This book celebrates the 25th anniversary of the first "Star Trek" television episode and traces the history of the show that has become an enduring legend—even the non-Trekkies can quote specific lines and characters from the original television series. The History of Trek chronicles "Star Trek" from its start in 1966 to its cancellation in 1969; discusses the lean years when "Star Trek" wasn't shown on television but legions of die hard fans kept interest in it still alive; covers the sequence of five successful movies (and includes the upcoming sixth one); and reviews "The Next Generation" television series, now entering its sixth season. Complete with Photographs, The History of Trek reveals the origins of the first series in interviews with the original cast and creative staff. It also takes readers behind the scenes of all six Star Trek movies, offers a wealth of Star Trek Trivia, and speculates on what the future may hold.

$14.95.....160 Pages
ISBN # 1-55698-309-3

THE MAN BETWEEN THE EARS:
STAR TREKS LEONARD NIMOY

James Van Hise

Based on his numerous interviews with Leonard Nimoy, Van Hise tells the story of the man as well as the entertainer.

This book chronicles the many talents of Leonard Nimoy from the beginning of his career in Boston to his latest starring work in the movie, Never Forget. His 25-year association with Star Trek is the centerpiece, but his work outside the Starship Enterprise is also covered, from such early efforts as Zombies of the Stratosphere to his latest directorial and acting work, and his stage debut in Vermont.

$14.95.....160 Pages
ISBN # 1-55698-304-2

COUCH POTATO INC.   5715 N. Balsam Rd   Las Vegas, NV 89130   (702)658-2090

Use Your Credit Card 24 HRS — Order toll Free From: **(800)444-2524** Ext 67

TREK: THE MAKING OF THE MOVIES
James Van Hise

TREK: THE MAKING OF THE MOVIES tells the complete story both on-screen and behind the scenes of the biggest STAR TREK adventures of all. Plus the story of the STAR TREK II that never happened and the aborted STAR TREK VI: STARFLEET ACADEMY.

$14.95.....160 Pages
ISBN # 1-55698-313-1

TREK: THE LOST YEARS
Edward Gross

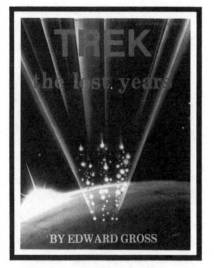

The tumultouos, behind-the-scenes saga of this modern day myth between the cancellation of the original series in 1969 and the announcement of the first movie ten years later. In addition, the text explores the scripts and treatments written throughout the 1970's, including every proposed theatrical feature and an episode guide for STAR TREK II, with comments from the writers whose efforts would ultimately never reach the screen.

This volume came together after years of research, wherein the author interviewed a wide variety of people involved with every aborted attempt at revival, from story editors to production designers to David Gautreaux, the actor signed to replace Leonard Nimoy; and had access to exclusive resource material, including memos and correspondences, as well as teleplays and script outlines.

$12.95.....132 Pages
ISBN # 1-55698-220-8

COUCH POTATO INC.   5715 N. Balsam Rd   Las Vegas, NV 89130   (702)658-2090

Use Your Credit Card 24 HRS — Order toll Free From: **(800)444-2524** Ext 67

BORING, BUT NECESSARY ORDERING INFORMATION

Payment:

Use our new 800 # and pay with your credit card or send check or money order directly to our address. All payments must be made in U.S. funds and please do not send cash.

Shipping:

We offer several methods of shipment. Sometimes a book can be delayed if we are temporarily out of stock. You should note whether you prefer us to ship the book as soon as available, send you a merchandise credit good for other goodies, or send your money back immediately.

Normal Post Office: $3.75 for the first book and $1.50 for each additional book. These orders are filled as quickly as possible. Shipments normally take 5 to 10 days, but allow up to 12 weeks for delivery.

Special UPS 2 Day Blue Label Service or Priority Mail: Special service is available for desperate Couch Potatoes. These books are shipped within 24 hours of when we receive the order and normally take 2 to 3 three days to get to you. The cost is $10.00 for the first book and $4.00 each additional book .

Overnight Rush Service: $20.00 for the first book and $10.00 each additional book.

U.s. Priority Mail: $6.00 for the first book and $3.00.each additional book.

Canada And Mexico: $5.00 for the first book and $3.00 each additional book.

Foreign: $6.00 for the first book and $3.00 each additional book.

Please list alternatives when available and please state if you would like a refund or for us to backorder an item if it is not in stock.

COUCH POTATO INC.   5715 N. Balsam Rd   Las Vegas, NV 89130   (702)658-2090

Use Your Credit Card 24 HRS — Order toll Free From: **(800)444-2524** Ext 67

ORDER FORM

_____ Trek Crew Book $9.95
_____ Best Of Enterprise Incidents $9.95
_____ Trek Fans Handbook $9.95
_____ Trek: The Next Generation $14.95
_____ The Man Who Created Star Trek: $12.95
_____ 25th Anniversary Trek Tribute $14.95
_____ History Of Trek $14.95
_____ The Man Between The Ears $14.95
_____ Trek: The Making Of The Movies $14.95
_____ Trek: The Lost Years $12.95
_____ Trek: The Unauthorized Next Generation $14.95
_____ New Trek Encyclopedia $19.95
_____ Making A Quantum Leap $14.95
_____ The Unofficial Tale Of Beauty And The Beast $14.95
_____ Complete Lost In Space $19.95
_____ ..doctor Who Encyclopedia: Baker $19.95
_____ Lost In Space Tribute Book $14.95
_____ Lost In Space With Irwin Allen $14.95
_____ Doctor Who: Baker Years $19.95
_____ Doctor Who: Pertwee Years $19.95
_____ Batmania Ii $14.95
_____ The Green Hornet $14.95 _____ Special Edition $16.95

_____ Number Six: The Prisoner Book $14.95
_____ Gerry Anderson: Supermarionation $17.95
_____ Addams Family Revealed $14.95
_____ Bloodsucker: Vampires At The Movies $14.95
_____ Dark Shadows Tribute $14.95
_____ Monsterland Fear Book $14.95
_____ The Films Of Elvis $14.95
_____ The Woody Allen Encyclopedia $14.95
_____ Paul Mccartney: 20 Years On His Own $9.95
_____ Yesterday: My Life With The Beatles $14.95
_____ Fab Films Of The Beatles $14.95
_____ 40 Years At Night: The Tonight Show $14.95

_____
_____ The La Lawbook $14.95
_____ Cheers: Where Everybody Knows Your Name $14.95

_____
_____ The Rockford Phile $14.95
_____ Encyclopedia Of Cartoon Superstars $14.95
_____ How To Create Animation $14.95
_____ How To Draw Art For Comic Books $14.95
_____ King And Barker:an Illustrated Guide $14.95
_____ King And Barker: An Illustrated Guide II $14.95

100% Satisfaction Guaranteed.

We value your support. You will receive a full refund as long as the copy of the book you are not happy with is received back by us in reasonable condition. No questions asked, except we would like to know how we failed you. Refunds and credits are given as soon as we receive back the item you do not want.

NAME:_____

STREET:_____

CITY:_____

STATE:_____

ZIP:_____

TOTAL:_____ SHIPPING_____

SEND TO: Couch Potato, Inc. 5715 N. Balsam Rd., Las Vegas, NV 89130